War and the Future
Italy, France and Britain at War

H. G. Wells

Alpha Editions

This edition published in 2024

ISBN 9789362993625

Design and Setting By
Alpha Editions
www.alphaedis.com
Email - info@alphaedis.com

As per information held with us this book is in Public Domain.
This book is a reproduction of an important historical work.
Alpha Editions uses the best technology to reproduce historical work
in the same manner it was first published to preserve its original nature.
Any marks or number seen are left intentionally to preserve.

Contents

THE PASSING OF THE EFFIGY	- 1 -
THE WAR IN ITALY (AUGUST, 1916)	- 17 -
I. THE ISONZO FRONT	- 18 -
II. THE MOUNTAIN WAR	- 23 -
III. BEHIND THE FRONT	- 29 -
THE WESTERN WAR (SEPTEMBER, 1916)	- 37 -
I. RUINS	- 38 -
II. THE GRADES OF WAR	- 44 -
III. THE WAR LANDSCAPE	- 52 -
IV. NEW ARMS FOR OLD ONES	- 60 -
V. TANKS	- 72 -
HOW PEOPLE THINK ABOUT THE WAR	- 81 -
I. DO THEY REALLY THINK AT ALL?	- 82 -
II. THE YIELDING PACIFIST AND THE CONSCIENTIOUS OBJECTOR	- 88 -
III. THE RELIGIOUS REVIVAL	- 96 -
IV. THE RIDDLE OF THE BRITISH	- 104 -
V. THE SOCIAL CHANGES IN PROGRESS	- 111 -
VI. THE ENDING OF THE WAR	- 123 -

THE PASSING OF THE EFFIGY

1

One of the minor peculiarities of this unprecedented war is the Tour of the Front. After some months of suppressed information—in which even the war correspondent was discouraged to the point of elimination—it was discovered on both sides that this was a struggle in which Opinion was playing a larger and more important part than it had ever done before. This wild spreading weed was perhaps of decisive importance; the Germans at any rate were attempting to make it a cultivated flower. There was Opinion flowering away at home, feeding rankly on rumour; Opinion in neutral countries; Opinion getting into great tangles of misunderstanding and incorrect valuation between the Allies. The confidence and courage of the enemy; the amiability and assistance of the neutral; the zeal, sacrifice, and serenity of the home population; all were affected. The German cultivation of opinion began long before the war; it is still the most systematic and, because of the psychological ineptitude of the Germans, it is probably the clumsiest. The French *Maison de la Presse* is certainly the best organisation in existence for making things clear, counteracting hostile suggestion, the British official organisations are comparatively ineffective; but what is lacking officially is very largely made up for by the good will and generous efforts of the English and American press. An interesting monograph might be written upon these various attempts of the belligerents to get themselves and their proceedings explained.

Because there is perceptible in these developments, quite over and above the desire to influence opinion, a very real effort to get things explained. It is the most interesting and curious—one might almost write touching—feature of these organisations that they do not constitute a positive and defined propaganda such as the Germans maintain. The German propaganda is simple, because its ends are simple; assertions of the moral elevation and loveliness of Germany; of the insuperable excellences of German Kultur, the Kaiser, and Crown Prince, and so forth; abuse of the "treacherous" English who allied themselves with the "degenerate" French and the "barbaric" Russians; nonsense about "the freedom of the seas"— the emptiest phrase in history—childish attempts to sow suspicion between the Allies, and still more childish attempts to induce neutrals and simple-minded pacifists of allied nationality to save the face of Germany by initiating peace negotiations. But apart from their steady record and reminder of German brutalities and German aggression, the press organisations of the Allies have none of this definiteness in their task. The aim of the national intelligence in each of the allied countries is not to exalt one's own nation and confuse and divide the enemy, but to get a real understanding with the peoples and spirits of a number of different nations, an understanding that will increase and become a fruitful and permanent understanding between the allied peoples. Neither the English, the Russians, the Italians, nor the French, to name only the bigger European allies, are concerned in setting up a legend, as the Germans are concerned in setting up a legend of themselves to impose upon mankind. They are reality dealers in this war, and the Germans are effigy mongers. Practically the Allies are saying each to one another, "Pray come to me and see for yourself that I am very much the human stuff that you are. Come and see that I am doing my best—and I think that is not so very bad a best...." And with that is something else still more subtle, something rather in the form of, "And please tell me what you think of me—and all this."

So we have this curious byplay of the war, and one day I find Mr. Nabokoff, the editor of the *Retch*, and Count Alexy Tolstoy, that writer of delicate short stories, and Mr. Chukovsky, the subtle critic, calling in upon me after braving the wintry seas to see the British fleet; M. Joseph Reinach follows them presently upon the same errand; and then appear photographs of Mr. Arnold Bennett wading in the trenches of Flanders, Mr. Noyes becomes discreetly indiscreet about what he has seen among the submarines, and Mr. Hugh Walpole catches things from Mr. Stephen Graham in the Dark Forest of Russia. All this is quite over and above such writing of facts at first hand as Mr. Patrick McGill and a dozen other real experiencing soldiers—not to mention the soldiers' letters Mr. James Milne has collected, or the unforgettable and immortal *Prisoner of War* of Mr. Arthur Green—or such admirable war correspondents' work as Mr. Philip Gibbs or Mr. Washburne has done. Some of us writers—I can answer for one—have made our Tour of the Fronts with a very understandable diffidence. For my own part I did not want to go. I evaded a suggestion that I should go in 1915. I travel badly, I speak French and Italian with incredible atrocity, and am an extreme Pacifist. I hate soldiering. And also I did not want to write anything "under instruction". It is largely owing to a certain stiffness in the composition of General Delme-Radcliffe is resolved that Italy shall not feel neglected by the refusal of the invitation from the Comando Supremo by anyone who from the perspective of Italy may seem to be a representative of British opinion. If Herbert Spencer had been alive General Radcliffe would have certainly made him come, travelling-hammock, ear clips and all—and I am not above confessing that I wish that Herbert Spencer was alive—for this purpose. I found Udine warm and gay with memories of Mr. Belloc, Lord Northcliffe, Mr. Sidney Low, Colonel Repington and Dr. Conan Doyle, and anticipating the arrival of Mr. Harold

Cox. So we pass, mostly in automobiles that bump tremendously over war roads, a cloud of witnesses each testifying after his manner. Whatever else has happened, we have all been photographed with invincible patience and resolution under the direction of Colonel Barberich in a sunny little court in Udine.

My own manner of testifying must be to tell what I have seen and what I have thought during this extraordinary experience. It has been my natural disposition to see this war as something purposeful and epic, as it is great, as an epoch, as "the War that will end War"—but of that last, more anon. I do not think I am alone in this inclination to a dramatic and logical interpretation. The caricatures in the French shops show civilisation (and particularly Marianne) in conflict with a huge and hugely wicked Hindenburg Ogre. Well, I come back from this tour with something not so simple as that. If I were to be tied down to one word for my impression of this war, I should say that this war is *Queer*. It is not like anything in a really waking world, but like something in a dream. It hasn't exactly that clearness of light against darkness or of good against ill. But it has the quality of wholesome instinct struggling under a nightmare. The world is not really awake. This vague appeal for explanations to all sorts of people, this desire to exhibit the business, to get something in the way of elucidation at present missing, is extraordinarily suggestive of the efforts of the mind to wake up that will sometimes occur at a deep crisis. My memory of this tour I have just made is full of puzzled-looking men. I have seen thousands of *poilus* sitting about in cafes, by the roadside, in tents, in trenches, thoughtful. I have seen Alpini sitting restfully and staring with speculative eyes across the mountain gulfs towards unseen and unaccountable enemies. I have seen trainloads of wounded staring out of the ambulance train windows as we passed. I have seen these dim intimations of questioning reflection in the strangest juxtapositions; in Malagasy soldiers resting for a spell among the big shells they were hoisting into trucks for the front, in a couple of khaki-clad Maoris sitting upon the step of a horse-van in Amiens station. It is always the same expression one catches, rather weary, rather sullen, inturned. The shoulders droop. The very outline is a note of interrogation. They look up as the privileged tourist of the front, in the big automobile or the reserved compartment, with his officer or so in charge, passes—importantly. One meets a pair of eyes that seems to say: "Perhaps *you* understand...."

"In which case——...?"

It is a part, I think, of this disposition to investigate what makes everyone collect "specimens" of the war. Everywhere the souvenir forces itself upon the attention. The homecoming permissionaire brings with him invariably a considerable weight of broken objects, bits of shell, cartridge clips, helmets; it is a peripatetic museum. It is as if he hoped for a clue. It is almost impossible, I have found, to escape these pieces in evidence. I am the least collecting of men, but I have brought home Italian cartridges, Austrian cartridges, the fuse of an Austrian shell, a broken Italian bayonet, and a note that is worth half a franc within the confines of Amiens. But a large heavy piece of exploded shell that had been thrust very urgently upon my attention upon the Carso I contrived to lose during the temporary confusion of our party by the arrival and explosion of another prospective souvenir in our close proximity. And two really very large and almost complete specimens of some species of *Ammonites* unknown to me, from the hills to the east of the Adige, partially wrapped in a back number of the *Corriere della Sera*, that were pressed upon me by a friendly officer, were unfortunately lost on the line between Verona and Milan through the gross negligence of a railway porter. But I doubt if they would have thrown any very conclusive light upon the war.

2

I avow myself an extreme Pacifist. I am against the man who first takes up the weapon. I carry my pacifism far beyond the ambiguous little group of British and foreign sentimentalists who pretend so amusingly to be socialists in the *Labour Leader*, whose conception of foreign policy is to give Germany now a peace that would be no more than a breathing time for a fresh outrage upon civilisation, and who would even make heroes of the crazy young assassins of the Dublin crime. I do not understand those people. I do not merely want to stop this war. I want to nail down war in its coffin. Modern war is an intolerable thing. It is not a thing to trifle with in this Urban District Council way, it is a thing to end forever. I have always hated it, so far that is as my imagination enabled me to realise it; and now that I have been seeing it, sometimes quite closely for a full month, I hate it more than ever. I never imagined a quarter of its waste, its boredom, its futility, its desolation. It is merely a destructive and dispersive instead of a constructive and accumulative industrialism. It is a gigantic, dusty, muddy, weedy, bloodstained silliness. It is the plain duty of every man to give his life and all that he has if by so doing he may help to end it. I hate Germany, which has thrust this experience upon mankind, as I hate some horrible infectious disease. The new war, the war on the modern level, is her invention and her crime. I perceive that on our side and in its broad outlines, this war is nothing more than a gigantic and heroic effort in sanitary engineering; an effort to remove German militarism from the life and regions it has invaded, and to bank it in and discredit and enfeeble it so that never more will it repeat its present preposterous and horrible efforts. All human affairs and all great affairs have their reservations and their complications, but that is the broad outline of the business as it has impressed itself on my mind and as I find it conceived in the mind of the average man of the reading class among the allied peoples, and as I find it understood in the judgement of honest and intelligent neutral observers.

It is my unshakeable belief that essentially the Allies fight for a permanent world peace, that primarily they do not make war but resist war, that has reconciled me to this not very congenial experience of touring as a spectator all agog to see, through the war zones. At any rate there was never any risk of my playing Balaam and blessing the enemy. This war is tragedy and sacrifice for most of the world, for the Germans it is simply the catastrophic outcome of fifty years of elaborate intellectual foolery. Militarism, Welt Politik, and here we are! What else *could* have happened, with Michael and his infernal War Machine in the very centre of Europe, but this tremendous disaster?

It is a disaster. It may be a necessary disaster; it may teach a lesson that could be learnt in no other way; but for all that, I insist, it remains waste, disorder, disaster.

There is a disposition, I know, in myself as well as in others, to wriggle away from this verity, to find so much good in the collapse that has come to the mad direction of Europe for the past half-century as to make it on the whole almost a beneficial thing. But at most I can find it in no greater good than the good of a nightmare that awakens the sleeper in a dangerous place to a realisation of the extreme danger of his sleep. Better had he been awake—or never there. In Venetia Captain Pirelli, whose task it was to keep me out of mischief in the war zone, was insistent upon the way in which all Venetia was being opened up by the new military roads; there has been scarcely a new road made in Venetia since Napoleon drove his straight, poplar-bordered highways through the land. M. Joseph Reinach, who was my companion upon the French front, was equally impressed by the stirring up and exchange of ideas in the villages due to the movement of the war. Charles Lamb's story of the discovery of roast pork comes into one's head with an effect of repartee. More than ideas are exchanged in the war zone, and it is doubtful how far the sanitary precautions of the military authorities avails against a considerable propaganda of disease. A more serious argument for the good of war is that it evokes heroic qualities that it has brought out almost incredible quantities of courage, devotion, and individual romance that did not show in the suffocating peace time that preceded the war. The reckless and beautiful zeal of the women in the British and French munition factories, for example, the gaiety and fearlessness of the common soldiers everywhere; these things have always been there—like champagne sleeping in bottles in a cellar. But was there any need to throw a bomb into the cellar?

I am reminded of a story, or rather of the idea for a story that I think I must have read in that curious collection of fantasies and observations, Hawthorne's *Note Book*. It was to be the story of a man who found life dull and his circumstances altogether mediocre. He had loved his wife, but now after all she seemed to be a very ordinary human being. He had begun life with high hopes—and life was commonplace. He was to grow fretful and restless. His discontent was to lead to some action, some irrevocable action; but upon the nature of that action I do not think the *Note Book* was very clear. It was to carry him in such a manner that he was to forget his wife. Then, when it was too late, he was to see her at an upper window, stripped and firelit, a glorious thing of light and loveliness and tragic intensity....

The elementary tales of the world are very few, and Hawthorne's story and Lamb's story are, after all, only variations upon the same theme. But can we poor human beings never realise our quality without destruction?

3

One of the larger singularities of the great war is its failure to produce great and imposing personalities, mighty leaders, Napoleons, Caesars. I would indeed make that the essential thing in my reckoning of the war. It is a drama without a hero; without countless incidental heroes no doubt, but no star part. Even the Germans, with a national predisposition for hero-cults and living still in an atmosphere of Victorian humbug, can produce nothing better than that timber image, Hindenburg.

It is not that the war has failed to produce heroes so much as that it has produced heroism in a torrent. The great man of this war is the common man. It becomes ridiculous to pick out particular names. There are too many true stories of splendid acts in the past two years ever to be properly set down. The V.C.'s and the palms do but indicate samples. One would need an encyclopaedia, a row of volumes, of the gloriousness of human impulses. The acts of the small men in this war dwarf all the pretensions of the Great Man. Imperatively these multitudinous heroes forbid the setting up of effigies. When I was a young man I imitated Swift and posed for cynicism; I will confess that now at fifty and greatly helped by this war, I have fallen in love with mankind.

But if I had to pick out a single figure to stand for the finest quality of the Allies' war, I should I think choose the figure of General Joffre. He is something new in history. He is leadership without vulgar ambition. He is the extreme antithesis to the Imperial boomster of Berlin. He is as it were the ordinary common sense of men, incarnate. He is the antithesis of the effigy.

By great good luck I was able to see him. I was delayed in Paris on my way to Italy, and my friend Captain Millet arranged for a visit to the French front at Soissons and put me in charge of Lieutenant de Tessin, whom I had met in England studying British social questions long before this war. Afterwards Lieutenant de Tessin took me to the great hotel—it still proclaims "*Restaurant*" in big black letters on the garden wall—which shelters the General Headquarters of France, and here I was able to see and talk to Generals Pelle and Castelnau as well as to General Joffre. They are three very remarkable and very different men. They have at least one thing in common; it is clear that not one of them has spent ten minutes in all his life in thinking of himself as a Personage or Great Man. They all have the effect of being active and able men doing an extremely complicated and difficult but extremely interesting job to the very best of their ability. With me they had all one quality in common. They thought I was interested in what they were doing, and they were quite prepared to treat me as an intelligent man of a different sort, and to show me as much as I could understand....

Let me confess that de Tessin had had to persuade me to go to Headquarters. Partly that was because I didn't want to use up even ten minutes of the time of the French commanders, but much more was it because I have a dread of Personages.

There is something about these encounters with personages—as if one was dealing with an effigy, with something tremendous put up to be seen. As one approaches they become remoter; great unsuspected crevasses are discovered. Across these gulfs one makes ineffective gestures. They do not meet you, they pose at you enormously. Sometimes there is something more terrible than dignity; there is condescension. They are affable. I had but recently had an encounter with an imported Colonial statesman, who was being advertised like a soap as the coming saviour of England. I was curious to meet him. I wanted to talk to him about all sorts of things that would have been profoundly interesting, as for example his impressions of the Anglican bishops. But I met a hoarding. I met a thing like a mask, something surrounded by touts, that was dully trying—as we say in London—to "come it" over me. He said he had heard of me. He had read *Kipps*. I intimated that though I had written *Kipps* I had continued to exist—but he did not see the point of that. I said certain things to him about the difference in complexity between political life in Great Britain and the colonies, that he was manifestly totally capable of understanding. But one could as soon have talked with one of the statesmen at Madame Tussaud's. An antiquated figure.

The effect of these French commanders upon me was quite different from my encounter with that last belated adventurer in the effigy line. I felt indeed that I was a rather idle and flimsy person coming into the presence of a tremendously compact and busy person, but I had none of that unpleasant sensation of a conventional role, of being expected to play the minute worshipper in the presence of the Great Image. I was so moved by the common humanity of them all that in each case I broke away from the discreet interpretations of de Tessin and talked to them directly in the strange dialect which I have inadvertently made for myself out of French, a disemvowelled speech of epicene substantives and verbs of incalculable moods and temperaments, "*Entente Cordiale.*" The talked back as if we had met in a club. General Pelle pulled my leg very gaily with some quotations from an article I had written upon the conclusion of the war. I think he found my accent and my idioms very refreshing. I had committed myself to a statement that Bloch has been justified in his theory that under modern conditions the defensive wins. There were excellent reasons, and General Pelle pointed them out, for doubting the applicability of this to the present war.

Both he and General Castelnau were anxious that I should see a French offensive sector as well as Soissons. Then I should understand. And since then I have returned from Italy and I have seen and I do understand. The Allied offensive was winning; that is to say, it was inflicting far greater losses than it experienced; it was steadily beating the spirit out of the German army and shoving it back towards Germany. Only peace can, I believe, prevent the western war ending in Germany. And it is the Frenchmen mainly who have worked out how to do it.

But of that I will write later. My present concern is with General Joffre as the antithesis of the Effigy. The effigy,

"*Thou Prince of Peace,*

Thou God of War,"

as Mr. Sylvester Viereck called him, prances on a great horse, wears a Wagnerian cloak, sits on thrones and talks of shining armour and "unser Gott." All Germany gloats over his Jovian domesticities; when I was last in Berlin the postcard shops were full of photographs of a sort of procession of himself and his sons, all with long straight noses and sidelong eyes. It is all dreadfully old-fashioned. General Joffre sits in a pleasant little sitting-room in a very ordinary little villa conveniently close to Headquarters. He sits among furniture that has no quality of pose at all, that is neither magnificent nor ostentatiously simple and hardy. He has dark, rather sleepy eyes under light eyelashes, eyes that glance shyly and a little askance at his interlocutor and then, as he talks, away—as if he did not want to be preoccupied by your attention. He has a broad, rather broadly modelled face, a soft voice, the sort of persuasive reasoning voice that many

Scotchmen have. I had a feeling that if he were to talk English he would do so with a Scotch accent. Perhaps somewhere I have met a Scotchman of his type. He sat sideways to his table as a man might sit for a gossip in a cafe.

He is physically a big man, and in my memory he grows bigger and bigger. He sits now in my memory in a room like the rooms that any decent people might occupy, like that vague room that is the background of so many good portraits, a great blue-coated figure with a soft voice and rather tired eyes, explaining very simply and clearly the difficulties that this vulgar imperialism of Germany, seizing upon modern science and modern appliances, has created for France and the spirit of mankind.

He talked chiefly of the strangeness of this confounded war. It was exactly like a sanitary engineer speaking of the unexpected difficulties of some particularly nasty inundation. He made little stiff horizontal gestures with his hands. First one had to build a dam and stop the rush of it, so; then one had to organise the push that would send it back. He explained the organisation of the push. They had got an organisation now that was working out most satisfactorily. Had I seen a sector? I had seen the sector of Soissons. Yes, but that was not now an offensive sector. I must see an offensive sector; see the whole method. Lieutenant de Tessin must see that that was arranged....

Neither he nor his two colleagues spoke of the Germans with either hostility or humanity. Germany for them is manifestly merely an objectionable Thing. It is not a nation, not a people, but a nuisance. One has to build up this great counter-thrust bigger and stronger until they go back. The war must end in Germany. The French generals have no such delusions about German science or foresight or capacity as dominates the smart dinner chatter of England. One knows so well that detestable type of English folly, and its voice of despair: "They *plan* everything. They foresee everything." This paralysing Germanophobia is not common among the French. The war, the French generals said, might take—well, it certainly looked like taking longer than the winter. Next summer perhaps. Probably, if nothing unforeseen occurred, before a full year has passed the job might be done. Were any surprises in store? They didn't seem to think it was probable that the Germans had any surprises in store.... The Germans are not an inventive people; they are merely a thorough people. One never knew for certain.

Is any greater contrast possible than between so implacable, patient, reasonable—and above all things *capable*—a being as General Joffre and the rhetorician of Potsdam, with his talk of German Might, of Hammer Blows and Hacking Through? Can there be any doubt of the ultimate issue between them?

There are stories that sound pleasantly true to me about General Joffre's ambitions after the war. He is tired; then he will be very tired. He will, he declares, spend his first free summer in making a tour of the waterways of France in a barge. So I hope it may be. One imagines him as sitting quietly on the crumpled remains of the last and tawdriest of Imperial traditions, with a fishing line in the placid water and a large buff umbrella overhead, the good ordinary man who does whatever is given to him to do—as well as he can. The power that has taken the great effigy of German imperialism by the throat is something very composite and complex, but if we personify it at all it is something more like General Joffre than any other single human figure I can think of or imagine.

If I were to set a frontispiece to a book about this War I would make General Joffre the frontispiece.

4

As we swung back along the dusty road to Paris at a pace of fifty miles an hour and upwards, driven by a helmeted driver with an aquiline profile fit to go upon a coin, whose merits were a little flawed by a childish and dangerous ambition to run over every cat he saw upon the road, I talked to de Tessin about this big blue-coated figure of Joffre, which is not so much a figure as a great generalisation of certain hitherto rather obscured French qualities, and of the impression he had made upon me. And from that I went on to talk about the Super Man, for this encounter had suddenly crystallised out a set of realisations that had been for some time latent in my mind.

How much of what follows I said to de Tessin at the time I do not clearly remember, but this is what I had in mind.

The idea of the superman is an idea that has been developed by various people ignorant of biology and unaccustomed to biological ways of thinking. It is an obvious idea that follows in the course of half an hour or so upon one's realisation of the significance of Darwinism. If man has evolved from something different, he must now be evolving onward into something sur-human. The species in the future will be different from the species of the past. So far at least our Nietzsches and Shaws and so on went right.

But being ignorant of the elementary biological proposition that modification of a species means really a secular change in its average, they jumped to a conclusion—to which the late Lord Salisbury also jumped years ago at a very memorable British Association meeting—that a species is modified by the sudden appearance of eccentric individuals here and there in the general mass who interbreed—preferentially. Helped by a streak of antic egotism in themselves, they conceived of the superman as a posturing personage, misunderstood by the vulgar, fantastic, wonderful. But the antic Personage, the thing I have called the Effigy, is not new but old, the oldest thing in history, the departing thing. It depends not upon the advance of the species but upon the uncritical hero-worship of the crowd. You may see the monster drawn twenty times the size of common men upon the oldest monuments of Egypt and Assyria. The true superman comes not as the tremendous personal entry of a star, but in the less dramatic form of a general increase of goodwill and skill and common sense. A species rises not by thrusting up peaks but by the brimming up as a flood does. The coming of the superman means not an epidemic of personages but the disappearance of the Personage in the universal ascent. That is the point overlooked by the megalomaniac school of Nietzsche and Shaw.

And it is the peculiarity of this war, it is the most reassuring evidence that a great increase in general ability and critical ability has been going on throughout the last century, that no isolated great personages have emerged. Never has there been so much ability, invention, inspiration, leadership; but the very abundance of good qualities has prevented our focusing upon those of any one individual. We all play our part in the realisation of God's sanity in the world, but, as the strange, dramatic end of Lord Kitchener has served to remind us, there is no single individual of all the allied nations whose death can materially affect the great destinies of this war.

In the last few years I have developed a religious belief that has become now to me as real as any commonplace fact. I think that mankind is still as it were collectively dreaming and hardly more awakened to reality than a very young child. It has these dreams that we express by the flags of nationalities and by strange loyalties and by irrational creeds and ceremonies, and its dreams at times become such nightmares as this war. But the time draws near when mankind will awake and the dreams will fade away, and then there will be no nationality in all the world but humanity, and no kind, no emperor, nor leader but the one God of mankind. This is my faith. I am as certain of this as I was in 1900 that men would presently fly. To me it is as if it must be so.

So that to me this extraordinary refusal of the allied nations under conditions that have always hitherto produced a Great Man to produce anything of the sort, anything that can be used as an effigy and carried about for the crowd to follow, is a fact of extreme significance and encouragement. It seems to me that the twilight of the half gods must have come, that we have reached the end of the age when men needed a Personal Figure about which they could rally. The Kaiser is perhaps the last of that long series of crowned and cloaked and semi-divine personages which has included Caesar and Alexander and Napoleon the First—and Third. In the light of the new time we see the emperor-god for the guy he is. In the August of 1914 he set himself up to be the paramount Lord of the World, and it will seem to the historian to come, who will know our dates so well and our feelings, our fatigues and efforts so little, it will seem a short period from that day to this, when the great figure already sways and staggers towards the bonfire.

5

I had the experience of meeting a contemporary king upon this journey. He was the first king I had ever met. The Potsdam figure—with perhaps some local exceptions behind the Gold Coast—is, with its collection of uniforms and its pomps and splendours, the purest survival of the old tradition of divine monarchy now that the Emperor at Pekin has followed the Shogun into the shadows. The modern type of king shows a disposition to intimate at the outset that he cannot help it, and to justify or at any rate utilise his exceptional position by sound hard work. It is an age of working kings, with the manners of private gentlemen. The King of Italy for example is far more accessible than was the late Pierpont Morgan or the late Cecil Rhodes, and he seems to keep a smaller court.

I went to see him from Udine. He occupied a moderate-sized country villa about half an hour by automobile from headquarters. I went over with General Radcliffe; we drove through the gates of the villa past a single sentinel in an ordinary infantry uniform, up to the door of the house, and the number of guards, servants, attendants, officials, secretaries, ministers and the like that I saw in that house were—I counted very carefully—four. Downstairs were three people, a tall soldier of the bodyguard in grey; an A.D.C., Captain Moreno, and Col. Matteoli, the minister of the household. I went upstairs to a drawing-room of much the same easy and generalised character as the one in which I had met General Joffre a few days before. I gave my hat to a second bodyguard, and as I did so a pleasantly smiling man appeared at the door of the study whom I thought at first must be some minister in attendance. I did not recognise him instantly because on the stamps and coins he is always in profile. He began to talk in excellent English about my journey, and I replied, and so talking we went into the study from which he had emerged. Then I realised I was talking to the king.

Addicted as I am to the cinematograph, in which the standard of study furniture is particularly rich and high, I found something very cooling and simple and refreshing in the sight of the king's study furniture. He sat down with me at a little useful writing table, and after asking me what I had seen in Italy and hearing what I had seen and what I was to see, he went on talking, very good talk indeed.

I suppose I did a little exceed the established tradition of courts by asking several questions and trying to get him to talk upon certain points as to which I was curious, but I perceived that he had had to carry on at least so much of the regal tradition as to control the conversation. He was, however, entirely un-posed. His talk reminded me somehow of Maurice Baring's books; it had just the same quick, positive understanding. And he had just the same detachment from the war as the French generals. He spoke of it—as one might speak of an inundation. And of its difficulties and perplexities.

Here on the Adriatic side there were political entanglements that by comparison made our western after-the-war problems plain sailing. He talked of the game of spellicans among the Balkan nationalities. How was that difficulty to be met? In Macedonia there were Turkish villages that were Christian and Bulgarians that were Moslem. There were families that changed the termination of their names from *ski* to *off* as Serbian or Bulgarian prevailed. I remarked that that showed a certain passion for peace, and that much of the mischief might be due to the propaganda of the great Powers. I have a prejudice against that blessed Whig "principle of nationality," but the King of Italy was not to be drawn into any statement about that. He left the question with his admission of its extreme complexity.

He went on to talk of the strange contrasts of war, of such things as the indifference of the birds to gunfire and desolation. One day on the Carso he had been near the newly captured Austrian trenches, and suddenly from amidst a scattered mass of Austrian bodies a quail had risen that had struck him as odd, and so too had the sight of a pack of cards and a wine flask on some newly-made graves. The ordinary life was a very *obstinate* thing....

He talked of the courage of modern men. He was astonished at the quickness with which they came to disregard shrapnel. And they were so quietly enduring when they were wounded. He had seen a lot of the wounded, and he had expected much groaning and crying out. But unless a man is hit in the head and goes mad he does not groan or scream! They are just brave. If you ask them how they feel it is always one of two things: either they say quietly that they are very bad or else they say there is nothing the matter....

He spoke as if these were mere chance observations, but everyone tells me that nearly every day the king is at the front and often under fire. He has taken more risks in a week than the Potsdam War Lord has taken since the war began. He keeps himself acutely informed upon every aspect of the war. He was a little inclined to fatalism, he confessed. There were two stories current of two families of four sons, in each three had been killed and in each there was an attempt to put the fourth in a place of comparative safety. In one case a general took the fourth son in as an attendant and embarked upon a ship that was immediately torpedoed; in the other the fourth son was killed by accident while he was helping to carry dinner in a rest camp. From those stories we came to the question whether the uneducated Italians were more superstitious than the uneducated English; the king thought they were much less so. That struck me as a novel idea. But then he thought that English rural people believe in witches and fairies.

I have given enough of this talk to show the quality of this king of the new dispensation. It was, you see, the sort of easy talk one might hear from fine-minded people anywhere. When we had done talking he came to the door of the study with me and shook hands and went back to his desk—with that gesture of return to work which is very familiar and sympathetic to a writer, and with no gesture of regality at all.

Just to complete this impression let me repeat a pleasant story about this king and our Prince of Wales, who recently visited the Italian front. The Prince is a source of anxiety on these visits; he has a very strong and very creditable desire to share the ordinary risks of war. He is keenly interested, and unobtrusively bent upon getting as near the fighting as line as possible. But the King of Italy was firm upon keeping him out of anything more than the most incidental danger. "We don't want any historical incidents here," he said. I think that might well become an historical phrase. For the life of the Effigy is a series of historical incidents.

6

Manifestly one might continue to multiply portraits of fine people working upon this great task of breaking and ending the German aggression, the German legend, the German effigy, and the effigy business generally; the thesis being that the Allies have no effigy. One might fill a thick volume with pictures of men up the scale and down working loyally and devotedly upon the war, to make this point clear that the essential king and the essential loyalty of our side is the commonsense of mankind.

There comes into my head as a picture at the other extreme of this series, a memory of certain trenches I visited on my last day in France. They were trenches on an offensive front; they were not those architectural triumphs, those homes from home, that grow to perfection upon the less active sections of the great line. They had been first made by men who had run rapidly forward with spade and rifle, stooping as they ran, who had dropped into the craters of big shells, who had organised these chiefly at night and dug the steep ditches sideways to join up into continuous trenches. Now they were pushing forward saps into No Man's Land, linking them across, and so continually creeping nearer to the enemy and a practicable jumping-off place for an attack. (It has been made since; the village at which I peeped was in our hands a week later.) These trenches were dug into a sort of yellowish sandy clay; the dug-outs were mere holes in the earth that fell in upon the clumsy; hardly any timber had been got up the line; a storm might flood them at any time a couple of feet deep and begin to wash the sides. Overnight they had been "strafed" and there had been a number of casualties; there were smashed rifles about and a smashed-up machine gun emplacement, and the men were dog-tired and many of them sleeping like logs, half buried in clay. Some slept on the firing steps. As one went along one became aware ever and again of two or three pairs of clay-yellow feet sticking out of a clay hole, and peering down one saw the shapes of men like rudely modelled earthen images of soldiers, motionless in the cave.

I came round the corner upon a youngster with an intelligent face and steady eyes sitting up on the firing step, awake and thinking. We looked at one another. There are moments when mind leaps to mind. It is natural for the man in the trenches suddenly confronted by so rare a beast as a middle-aged civilian with an enquiring expression, to feel oneself something of a spectacle and something generalised. It is natural for the civilian to look rather in the vein of saying, "Well, how do you take it?" As I pushed past him we nodded slightly with an effect of mutual understanding. And we said with our nods just exactly what General Joffre had said with his horizontal gestures of the hand and what the King of Italy conveyed by his friendly manner; we said to each other that here was the trouble those Germans had brought upon us and here was the task that had to be done.

Our guide to these trenches was a short, stocky young man, a cob; with a rifle and a tight belt and projecting skirts and a helmet, a queer little figure that, had you seen it in a picture a year or so before the war, you would most certainly have pronounced Chinese. He belonged to a Northumbrian battalion; it does not matter exactly which. As we returned from this front line, trudging along the winding path through the barbed wire tangles before the smashed and captured German trench that had been taken a fortnight before, I fell behind my guardian captain and had a brief conversation wit this individual. He was a lad in the early twenties, weather-bit and with bloodshot eyes. He was, he told me, a miner. I asked my stock question in such cases, whether he would go back to the old work after the war. He said he would, and then added—with the events of overnight on his mind: "If A'hm looky."

Followed a little silence. Then I tried my second stock remark for such cases. One does not talk to soldiers at the front in this war of Glory or the "Empire on which the sun never sets" or "the meteor flag of England" or of King and Country or any of those fine old headline things. On the desolate path that winds about amidst the shell craters and the fragments and the red-rusted wire, with the silken shiver of passing shells in the air and the blue of the lower sky continually breaking out into eddying white puffs, it is wonderful how tawdry such panoplies of the effigy appear. We knew that we and our allies are upon a greater, graver, more fundamental business than that sort of thing now. We are very near the waking point.

"Well," I said, "it's got to be done."

"Aye," he said, easing the strap of his rifle a little; "it's got to be done."

THE WAR IN ITALY (AUGUST, 1916)

I. THE ISONZO FRONT

1

My first impressions of the Italian war centre upon Udine. So far I had had only a visit to Soissons on an exceptionally quiet day and the sound of a Zeppelin one night in Essex for all my experience of actual warfare. But my bedroom at the British mission in Udine roused perhaps extravagant expectations. There were holes in the plaster ceiling and wall, betraying splintered laths, holes, that had been caused by a bomb that had burst and killed several people in the little square outside. Such excitements seem to be things of the past now in Udine. Udine keeps itself dark nowadays, and the Austrian sea-planes, which come raiding the Italian coast country at night very much in the same aimless, casually malignant way in which the Zeppelins raid England, apparently because there is nothing else for them to do, find it easier to locate Venice.

My earlier rides in Venetia began always with the level roads of the plain, roads frequently edged by watercourses, with plentiful willows beside the road, vines and fields of Indian corn and suchlike lush crops. Always quite soon one came to some old Austrian boundary posts; almost everywhere the Italians are fighting upon what is technically enemy territory, but nowhere does it seem a whit less Italian than the plain of Lombardy. When at last I motored away from Udine to the northern mountain front I passed through Campo-Formio and saw the white-faced inn at which Napoleon dismembered the ancient republic of Venice and bartered away this essential part of Italy into foreign control. It just gravitates back now—as though there had been no Napoleon.

And upon the roads and beside them was the enormous equipment of a modern army advancing. Everywhere I saw new roads being made, railways pushed up, vast store dumps, hospitals; everywhere the villages swarmed with grey soldiers; everywhere our automobile was threading its way and taking astonishing risks among interminable processions of motor lorries, strings of ambulances or of mule carts, waggons with timber, waggons with wire, waggons with men's gear, waggons with casks, waggons discreetly veiled, columns of infantry, cavalry, batteries *en route*. Every waggon that goes up full comes back empty, and many wounded were coming down and prisoners and troops returning to rest. Goritzia had been taken a week or so before my arrival; the Isonzo had been crossed and the Austrians driven back across the Carso for several miles; all the resources of Italy seemed to be crowding up to make good these gains and gather strength for the next thrust. The roads under all this traffic remained wonderful; gangs of men were everywhere repairing the first onset of wear, and Italy is the most fortunate land in the world for road metal; her mountains are solid road metal, and in this Venetian plain you need but to scrape through a yard of soil to find gravel.

One travelled through a choking dust under the blue sky, and above the steady incessant dusty succession of lorry, lorry, lorry, lorry that passed one by, one saw, looking up, the tree tops, house roofs, or the solid Venetian campanile of this or that wayside village. Once as we were coming out of the great grey portals of that beautiful old relic of a former school of fortification, Palmanova, the traffic became suddenly bright yellow, and for a kilometre or so we were passing nothing but Sicilian mule carts loaded with hay. These carts seem as strange among the grey shapes of modern war transport as a Chinese mandarin in painted silk would be. They are the most individual of things, all two-wheeled, all bright yellow and the same size it is true, but upon each there are they gayest of little paintings, such paintings as one sees in England at times upon an ice-cream barrow. Sometimes the picture will present a scriptural subject, sometimes a scene of opera, sometimes a dream landscape or a trophy of fruits or flowers, and the harness—now much out of repair—is studded with brass. Again and again I have passed strings of these gay carts; all Sicily must be swept of them.

Through the dust I came to Aquileia, which is now an old cathedral, built upon the remains of a very early basilica, standing in a space in a scattered village. But across this dusty space there was carried the head of the upstart Maximinus who murdered Alexander Severus, and later Aquileia brought Attila near to despair. Our party alighted; we inspected a very old mosaic floor which has been uncovered since the Austrian retreat. The Austrian priests have gone too, and their Italian successors are already tracing out a score of Roman traces that it was the Austrian custom to minimise. Captain Pirelli refreshed my historical memories; it was rather like leaving a card on Gibbon *en route* for contemporary history.

By devious routes I went on to certain batteries of big guns which had played their part in hammering the Austrian left above Monfalcone across an arm of the Adriatic, and which were now under orders to shift and move up closer. The battery was the most unobtrusive of batteries; its one desire seemed to be to appear a simple piece of woodland in the eye of God and the aeroplane. I went about the network of railways and paths under the trees that a modern battery requires, and came presently upon a great gun that even at the first glance seemed a little less carefully hidden than its fellows. Then I saw that it was a most ingenious dummy made of a tree and logs and so forth. It was in the emplacement of a real gun that had been located; it had its painted sandbags about it just the same, and it felt itself so entirely a part of the battery that whenever its companions fired t burnt a flash and kicked up a dust. It was an excellent example of the great art of camouflage which this war has developed.

I went on through the wood to a shady observation post high in a tree, into which I clambered with my guide. I was able from this position to get a very good idea of the lie of the Italian eastern front. I was in the delta of the Isonzo. Directly in front of me were some marshes and the extreme tip of the Adriatic Sea, at the head of which was Monfalcone, now in Italian hands. Behind Monfalcone ran the red ridge of the Carso, of which the Italians had just captured the eastern half. Behind this again rose the mountains to the east of the Isonzo which the Austrians still held. The Isonzo came towards me from out of the mountains, in a great westward curve. Fifteen or sixteen miles away where it emerged from the mountains lay the pleasant and prosperous town of Goritzia, and at the westward point of the great curve was Sagrado with its broken bridge. The battle of Goritzia was really not fought at Goritzia at all. What happened was the brilliant and bloody storming of Mounts Podgora and Sabotino on the western side of the river above Goritzia, and simultaneously a crossing at Sagrado below Goritzia and a magnificent rush up the plateau and across the plateau of the Carso. Goritzia itself was not organised for defence, and the Austrians were so surprised by the rapid storm of the mountains to the north-west of it and of the Carso to the south-east, that they made no fight in the town itself.

As a consequence when I visited it I found it very little injured—compared, that is, with such other towns as have been fought through. Here and there the front of a house has been knocked in by an Austrian shell, or a lamp-post prostrated. But the road bridge had suffered a good deal; its iron parapet was twisted about by shell bursts and interwoven with young trees and big boughs designed to screen the passer-by from the observation of the Austrian gunners upon Monte Santo. Here and there were huge holes through which one could look down upon the blue trickles of water in the stony river bed far below. The driver of our automobile displayed what seemed to me an extreme confidence in the margins of these gaps, but his confidence was justified. At Sagrado the bridge had been much more completely demolished; no effort had been made to restore the horizontal roadway, but one crossed by a sort of timber switchback that followed the ups and downs of the ruins.

It is not in these places that one must look for the real destruction of modern war. The real fight on the left of Goritzia went through the village of Lucinico up the hill of Podgora. Lucinico is nothing more than a heap of grey stones; except for a bit of the church wall and the gable end of a house one cannot even speak of it as ruins. But in one place among the rubble I saw the splintered top and a leg of a grand piano. Podgora hill, which was no doubt once neatly terraced and cultivated, is like a scrap of landscape from some airless, treeless planet. Still more desolate was the scene upon the Carso to the right (south) of Goritzia. Both San Martino and Doberdo are destroyed beyond the limits of ruination. The Carso itself is a waterless upland with but a few bushy trees; it must always have been a desolate region, but now it is an indescribable wilderness of shell craters, smashed-up Austrian trenches, splintered timber, old iron, rags, and that rusty thorny vileness of man's invention, worse than all the thorns and thickets of nature, barbed wire. There are no dead visible; the wounded have been cleared away; but about the trenches and particularly near some of the dug-outs there was a faint repulsive smell....

Yet into this wilderness the Italians are now thrusting a sort of order. The German is a wonderful worker, they say on the Anglo-French front that he makes his trenches by way of resting, but I doubt if he can touch the Italian at certain forms of toil. All the way up to San Martino and beyond, swarms of workmen were making one of those carefully graded roads that the Italians make better than any other people. Other swarms were laying water-pipes. For upon the Carso there are neither roads nor water, and before the Italians can thrust farther both must be brought up to the front.

As we approached San Martino an Austrian aeroplane made its presence felt overhead by dropping a bomb among the tents of some workmen, in a little scrubby wood on the hillside near at hand. One heard the report and turned to see the fragments flying and the dust. Probably they got someone. And then, after a little pause, the encampment began to spew out men; here, there and everywhere they appeared among the tents, running like rabbits at evening-time, down the hill. Soon after and probably in connection with this signal, Austrian shells began to come over. They do not use shrapnel because the rocky soil of Italy makes that unnecessary. They fire a sort of shell that goes bang and releases a cloud of smoke overhead, and then drops a parcel of high explosive that bursts on the ground. The ground leaps into red dust and smoke. But these things are now to be seen on the cinema. Forthwith the men working on the road about us begin to down tools and make for the shelter trenches, a long procession going at a steady but resolute walk. Then like a blow in the chest came the bang of a big Italian gun somewhere close at hand....

Along about four thousand miles of the various fronts this sort of thing was going on that morning....

2

This Carso front is the practicable offensive front of Italy. From the left wing on the Isonzo along the Alpine boundary round to the Swiss boundary there is mountain warfare like nothing else in the world; it is warfare that pushes the boundary backward, but it is mountain warfare that will not, for so long a period that the war will be over first, hold out any hopeful prospects of offensive movements on a large scale against Austria or Germany. It is a short distance as the crow flies from Rovereto to Munich, but not as the big gun travels. The Italians, therefore, as their contribution to the common effort, are thrusting rather eastwardly towards the line of the Julian Alps through Carinthia and Carniola. From my observation post in the tree near Monfalcone I saw Trieste away along the coast to my right. It looked scarcely as distant as Folkestone from Dungeness. The Italian advanced line is indeed scarcely ten miles from Trieste. But the Italians are not, I think, going to Trieste just yet. That is not the real game now. They are playing loyally with the Allies for the complete defeat of the Central Powers, and that is to be achieved striking home into Austria. Meanwhile there is no sense in knocking Trieste to pieces, or using Italians instead of Austrian soldiers to garrison it.

II. THE MOUNTAIN WAR

1

The mountain warfare of Italy is extraordinarily unlike that upon any other front. From the Isonzo to the Swiss frontier we are dealing with high mountains, cut by deep valleys between which there is usually no practicable lateral communication. Each advance must have the nature of an unsupported shove along a narrow channel, until the whole mountain system, that is, is won, and the attack can begin to deploy in front of the passes. Geographically Austria has the advantage. She had the gentler slope of the mountain chains while Italy has the steep side, and the foresight of old treaties has given her deep bites into what is naturally Italian territory; she is far nearer the Italian plain than Italy is near any practicable fighting ground for large forces; particularly is this the case in the region of the Adige valley and Lake Garda.

The legitimate war, so to speak, in this region is a mountaineering war. The typical position is roughly as follows. The Austrians occupy valley A which opens northward; the Italians occupy valley B which opens southward. The fight is for the crest between A and B. The side that wins that crest gains the power of looking down into, firing into and outflanking the positions of the enemy valley. In most cases it is the Italians now who are pressing, and if the reader will examine a map of the front and compare it with the official reports he will soon realise that almost everywhere the Italians are up to the head of the southward valleys and working over the crests so as to press down upon the Austrian valleys. But in the Trentino the Austrians are still well over the crest on the southward slopes. When I was in Italy they still held Rovereto.

Now it cannot be said that under modern conditions mountains favour either the offensive or the defensive. But they certainly make operations far more deliberate than upon a level. An engineered road or railway in an Alpine valley is the most vulnerable of things; its curves and viaducts may be practically demolished by shell fire or swept by shrapnel, although you hold the entire valley except for one vantage point. All the mountains round about a valley must be won before that valley is safe for the transport of an advance. But on the other hand a surprise capture of some single mountain crest and the hoisting of one gun into position there may block the retreat of guns and material from a great series of positions. Mountain surfaces are extraordinarily various and subtle. You may understand Picardy on a map, but mountain warfare is three-dimensional. A struggle may go on for weeks or months consisting of apparently separate and incidental skirmishes, and then suddenly a whole valley organisation may crumble away in retreat or disaster. Italy is gnawing into the Trentino day by day, and particularly around by her right wing. At no time I shall be surprised to see a sudden lunge forward on that front, and hear a tale of guns and prisoners. This will not mean that she has made a sudden attack, but that some system of Austrian positions has collapsed under her continual pressure.

Such briefly is the *idea* of mountain struggle. Its realities, I should imagine, are among the strangest and most picturesque in all this tremendous world conflict. I know nothing of the war in the east, of course, but there are things here that must be hard to beat. Happily they will soon get justice done to them by an abler pen than mine. I hear that Kipling is to follow me upon this ground; nothing can be imagined more congenial to his extraordinary power of vivid rendering than this struggle against cliffs, avalanches, frost and the Austrian.

To go the Italian round needs, among other things, a good head. Everywhere it has been necessary to make roads where hitherto there have been only mule tracks or no tracks at all; the roads are often still in the making, and the automobile of the war tourist skirts precipices and takes hairpin bends upon tracks of loose metal not an inch too broad for the operation, or it floats for a moment over the dizzy edge while a train of mule transport blunders by. The unruly imagination of man's heart (which is "only evil continually") speculates upon what would be the consequences of one good bump from the wheel of a mule cart. Down below, the trees that one sees through a wisp of cloud look far too small and spiky and scattered to hold out much hope for a fallen man of letters. And at the high positions they are too used to the vertical life to understand the secret feelings of the visitor from the horizontal. General Bompiani, whose writings are well known to all English students of military matters, showed me the Gibraltar he is making of a great mountain system east of the Adige.

"Let me show you," he said, and flung himself on to the edge of the precipice into exactly the position of a lady riding side-saddle. "You will find it more comfortable to sit down."

But anxious as I am abroad not to discredit my country by unseemly exhibitions I felt unequal to such gymnastics without a proper rehearsal at a lower level. I seated myself carefully at a yard (perhaps it was a couple of yards) from the edge, advanced on my trousers without dignity to the verge, and so with an effort thrust my legs over to dangle in the crystalline air.

"That," proceeded General Bompiani, pointing with a giddy flourish of his riding whip, "is Monte Tomba."

I swayed and half-extended my hand towards him. But he was still there—sitting, so to speak, on the half of himself.... I was astonished that he did not disappear abruptly during his exposition....

2

The fighting man in the Dolomites has been perhaps the most wonderful of all these separate campaigns. I went up by automobile as far as the clambering new road goes up the flanks of Tofana No. 2; thence for a time by mule along the flank of Tofana No. 1, and thence on foot to the vestiges of the famous Castelletto.

The aspect of these mountains is particularly grim and wicked; they are worn old mountains, they tower overhead in enormous vertical cliffs of sallow grey, with the square jointings and occasional clefts and gullies, their summits are toothed and jagged; the path ascends and passes round the side of the mountain upon loose screes, which descend steeply to a lower wall of precipices. In the distance rise other harsh and desolate-looking mountain masses, with shining occasional scars of old snow. Far below is a bleak valley of stunted pine trees through which passes the road of the Dolomites.

As I ascended the upper track two bandages men were coming down on led mules. It was mid-August, and they were suffering from frostbite. Across the great gap between the summits a minute traveller with some provisions was going up by wire to some post upon the crest. For everywhere upon the icy pinnacles are observation posts directing the fire of the big guns on the slopes below, or machine-gun stations, or little garrisons that sit and wait through the bleak days. Often they have no link with the world below but a precipitous climb or a "teleferic" wire. Snow and frost may cut them off absolutely for weeks from the rest of mankind. The sick and wounded must begin their journey down to help and comfort in a giddy basket that swings down to the head of the mule track below.

Originally all these crests were in Austrian hands; they were stormed by the Alpini under almost incredible conditions. For fifteen days, for example, they fought their way up these screes on the flanks of Tofana No. 2 to the ultimate crags, making perhaps a hundred metres of ascent each day, hiding under rocks and in holes in the daylight and receiving fresh provisions and ammunition and advancing by night. They were subjected to rifle fire, machine-gun fire and bombs of a peculiar sort, big iron balls of the size of a football filled with explosive that were just flung down the steep. They dodged flares and star shells. At one place they went up a chimney that would be far beyond the climbing powers of any but a very active man. It must have been like storming the skies. The dead and wounded rolled away often into inaccessible ravines. Stray skeletons, rags of uniform, fragments of weapons, will add to the climbing interest of these gaunt masses for many years to come. In this manner it was that Tofana No. 2 was taken.

Now the Italians are organising this prize, and I saw winding up far above me on the steep grey slope a multitudinous string of little things that looked like black ants, each carrying a small bright yellow egg. They were mules bringing back balks of timber....

But one position held out invincibly; this was the Castelletto, a great natural fortress of rock standing out at an angle of the mountain in such a position that it commanded the Italian communications (the Dolomite road) in the valley below, and rendered all their positions uncomfortable and insecure. This obnoxious post was practically inaccessible either from above or below, and it barred the Italians even from looking into the Val Travenanzes which it defended. It was, in fact, an impregnable position, and against it was pitted the invincible 5th Group of the Alpini. It was the old problem of the irresistible force in conflict with the immovable object. And the outcome has been the biggest military mine in all history.

The business began in January, 1916, with surveys of the rock in question. The work of surveying for excavations, never a very simple one, becomes much more difficult when the site is occupied by hostile persons with machine guns. In March, as the winter's snows abated, the boring machinery began to arrive, by mule as far as possible and then by hand. Altogether about half a kilometre of gallery had to be made to the mine chamber, and meanwhile the explosive was coming up load by load and resting first here, then there, in discreetly chosen positions. There were at the last thirty-five tons of it in the inner chamber. And while the boring machines bored and the work went on, Lieutenant Malvezzi was carefully working out the problem of "il massimo effetto dirompimento" and deciding exactly how to pack and explode his little hoard. On the eleventh of July, at 3.30, as he rejoices to state in his official report, "the mine responded perfectly both in respect of the calculations made and of the practical effects," that is to say, the Austrians were largely missing and the Italians were in possession of the crater of the Castelletto and looking down the Val Travenanzes from which they had been barred for so long. Within a month things had been so tidied up, and secured by further excavations and sandbags against hostile fire, that even a middle-aged English writer, extremely fagged and hot and breathless, could enjoy the same privilege. All this, you must understand, had gone on at a level to which the ordinary tourist rarely climbs, in a rarefied, chest-tightening atmosphere, with wisps of clouds floating in the clear air below and club-huts close at hand....

Among these mountains avalanches are frequent; and they come down regardless of human strategy. In many cases the trenches cross avalanche tracks; they and the men in them are periodically swept away and periodically replaced. They are positions that must be held; if the Italians will not face such sacrifices, the Austrians will. Avalanches and frostbite have slain and disabled their thousands; they have accounted perhaps for as many Italians in this austere and giddy campaign as the Austrians....

3

It seems to be part of the stern resolve of Fate that this, the greatest of wars, shall be the least glorious; it is manifestly being decided not by victories but by blunders. It is indeed a history of colossal stupidities. Among the most decisive of these blunders, second only perhaps of the blunder of the Verdun attack and far outshining the wild raid of the British towards Bagdad, was the blunder of the Trentino offensive. It does not need the equipment of a military expert, it demands only quite ordinary knowledge and average intelligence, to realise the folly of that Austrian adventure. There is some justification for a claim that the decisive battle of the war was fought upon the soil of Italy. There is still more justification for saying that it might have been.

There was only one good point about the Austrian thrust. No one could have foretold it. And it did so completely surprise the Italians as to catch them without any prepared line of positions in the rear. On the very eve of the big Russian offensive, the Austrians thrust eighteen divisions hard at the Trentino frontier. The Italian posts were then in Austrian territory; they held on the left wing and the right, but they were driven by the sheer weight of men and guns in the centre; they lost guns and prisoners because of the difficulty of mountain retreats to which I have alluded, and the Austrians pouring through reached not indeed the plain of Venetia, but to the upland valleys immediately above it, to Asiago and Arsiero. They probably saw the Venetian plain through gaps in the hills, but they were still separated from it even at Arsiero by what are mountains to an English eye, mountains as high as Snowdon. But the Italians of such beautiful old places and Vicenza, Marostica, and Bassano could watch the Austrian shells bursting on the last line of hills above the plain, and I have no doubt they felt extremely uneasy.

As one motors through these ripe and beautiful towns and through the rich valleys that link them—it is a smiling land abounding in old castles and villas, Vicenza is a rich museum of Palladio's architecture and Bassano is full of irreplaceable painted buildings—one feels that the things was a narrow escape, but from the military point of view it was merely an insane escapade. The Austrians had behind them—and some way behind them—one little strangulated railway and no good pass road; their right was held at

Pasubio, their left was similarly bent back. In front of them was between twice and three times their number of first class troops, with an unlimited equipment. If they had surmounted that last mountain crest they would have come down to almost certain destruction in the plain. They could never have got back. For a time it was said that General Cadorna considered that possibility. From the point of view of purely military considerations, the Trentino offensive should perhaps have ended in the capitulation of Vicenza.

I will confess I am glad it did not do so. This tour of the fronts has made me very sad and weary with a succession of ruins. I can bear no more ruins unless they are the ruins of Dusseldorf, Cologne, Berlin, or suchlike modern German city. Anxious as I am to be a systematic Philistine, to express my preference for Marinetti over the Florentine British and generally to antagonise aesthetic prigs, I rejoiced over that sunlit land as one might rejoice over a child saved from beasts.

On the hills beyond Schio I walked out through the embrasure of a big gun in a rock gallery, and saw the highest points upon the hillside to which the Austrian infantry clambered in their futile last attacks. Below me were the ruins of Arsiero and Velo d'Astico recovered, and across the broad valley rose Monte Cimone with the Italian trenches upon its crest and the Austrians a little below to the north. A very considerable bombardment was going on and it reverberated finely. (It is only among mountains that one hears anything that one can call the thunder of guns. The heaviest bombardments I heard in France sounded merely like Brock's benefit on a much large scale, and disappointed me extremely.) As I sat and listened to the uproar and watched the shells burst on Cimone and far away up the valley over Castelletto above Pedescala, Captain Pirelli pointed out the position of the Austrian frontier. I doubt if the English people realise that the utmost depth to which this great Trentino offensive, which exhausted Austria, wasted the flower of the Hungarian army and led directly to the Galician disasters and the intervention of Rumania, penetrated into Italian territory was about six miles.

III. BEHIND THE FRONT

1

I have a peculiar affection for Verona and certain things in Verona. Italians must forgive us English this little streak of impertinent proprietorship in the beautiful things of their abundant land. It is quite open to them to revenge themselves by professing a tenderness for Liverpool or Leeds. It was, for instance, with a peculiar and personal indignation that I saw where an Austrian air bomb had killed five-and-thirty people in the Piazza Erbe. Somehow in that jolly old place, a place that have very much of the quality of a very pretty and cheerful old woman, it seemed exceptionally an outrage. And I made a special pilgrimage to see how it was with that monument of Can Grande, the equestrian Scaliger with the sidelong grin, for whom I confess a ridiculous admiration. Can Grande, I rejoice to say, has retired into a case of brickwork, surmounted by a steep roof of thick iron plates; no aeroplane exists to carry bombs enough to smash that covering; there he will smile securely in the darkness until peace comes again.

All over Venetia the Austrian seaplanes are making the same sort of idiot raid on lighted places that the Zeppelins have been making over England. These raids do no effective military work. What conceivable military advantage can there be in dropping bombs into a marketing crowd? It is a sort of anti-Teutonic propaganda by the Central Powers to which they seem to have been incited by their own evil genius. It is as if they could convince us that there is an essential malignity in Germans, that until the German powers are stamped down into the mud they will continue to do evil things. All of the Allies have borne the thrusting and boasting of Germany with exemplary patience for half a century; England gave her Heligoland and stood out of the way of her colonial expansion, Italy was a happy hunting ground for her business enterprise, France had come near resignation on the score of Alsace-Lorraine. And then over and above the great outrage of the war come these incessant mean-spirited atrocities. A great and simple wickedness it is possible to forgive; the war itself, had it been fought greatly by Austria and Germany, would have made no such deep and enduring breach as these silly, futile assassinations have down between the Austro-Germans and the rest of the civilised world. One great misdeed is a thing understandable and forgivable; what grows upon the consciousness of the world is the persuasion that here we fight not a national sin but a national insanity; that we dare not leave the German the power to attack other nations any more for ever....

Venice has suffered particularly from this ape-like impulse to hurt and terrorise enemy non-combatants. Venice has indeed suffered from this war far more than any other town in Italy. Her trade has largely ceased; she has no visitors. I woke up on my way to Udine and found my train at Venice with an hour to spare; after much examining and stamping of my passport I was allowed outside the station wicket to get coffee in the refreshment room and a glimpse of a very sad and silent Grand Canal. There was nothing doing; a black despondent remnant of the old crowd of gondolas browsed dreamily among against the quay to stare at me the better. The empty palaces seemed to be sleeping in the morning sunshine because it was not worth while to wake up....

2

Except in the case of Venice, the war does not seem as yet to have made nearly such a mark upon life in Italy as it has in England or provincial France. People speak of Italy as a poor country, but that is from a banker's point of view. In some respects she is the richest country on earth, and in the matter of staying power I should think she is better off than any other belligerent. She produces food in abundance everywhere; her women are agricultural workers, so that the interruption of food production by the war has been less serious in Italy than in any other part of Europe. In peace time, she has constantly exported labour; the Italian worker has been a seasonal emigrant to America, north and south, to Switzerland, Germany and the south of France. The cessation of this emigration has given her great reserves of man power, so that she has carried on her admirable campaign with less interference with her normal economic life than any other power. The first person I spoke to upon the platform at Modane was a British officer engaged in forwarding Italian potatoes to the British front in France. Afterwards, on my return, when a little passport irregularity kept me for half a day in Modane, I went for a walk with him along the winding pass road that goes down into France. "You see hundreds and hundreds of new Fiat cars," he remarked, "along here—going up to the French front."

But there is a return trade. Near Paris I saw scores of thousands of shells piled high to go to Italy....

I doubt if English people fully realise either the economic sturdiness or the political courage of their Italian ally. Italy is not merely fighting a first-class war in first-class fashion but she is doing a big, dangerous, generous and far-sighted thing in fighting at all. France and England were obliged to fight; the necessity was as plain as daylight. The participation of Italy demanded a remoter wisdom. In the long run she would have been swallowed up economically and politically by Germany if she had not fought; but that was not a thing staring her plainly in the face as the danger, insult and challenge stared France and England in the face. What did stare her in the face was not merely a considerable military and political risk, but the rupture of very close financial and commercial ties. I found thoughtful men talking everywhere I have been in Italy of two things, of the Jugo-Slav riddle and of the question of post war finance. So far as the former matter goes, I think the Italians are set upon the righteous solution of all such riddles, they are possessed by an intelligent generosity. They are clearly set upon deserving Jugo-Slav friendship; they understand the plain necessity of open and friendly routes towards Roumania. It was an Italian who set out to explain to me that Fiume must be at least a free port; it would be wrong and foolish to cut the trade of Hungary off from the Mediterranean. But the banking puzzle is a more intricate and puzzling matter altogether than the possibility of trouble between Italian and Jugo-Slav.

I write of these things with the simplicity of an angel, but without an angelic detachment. Here are questions into which one does not so much rush as get reluctantly pushed. Currency and banking are dry distasteful questions, but it is clear that they are too much in the hands of mystery-mongers; it is as much the duty of anyone who talks and writes of affairs, it is as much the duty of every sane adult, to bring his possibly poor and unsuitable wits to bear upon these things, as it is for him to vote or enlist or pay his taxes. Behind the simple ostensible spectacle of Italy recovering the unredeemed Italy of the Trentino and East Venetia, goes on another drama. Has Italy been sinking into something rather hard to define called "economic slavery"? Is she or is she not escaping from that magical servitude? Before this question has been under discussion for a minute comes a name—for a time I was really quite unable to decide whether it is the name of the villain in the piece or of the maligned heroine, or a secret society or a gold mine, or a pestilence or a delusion—the name of the *Banca Commerciale Italiana*.

Banking in a country undergoing so rapid and vigorous an economic development as Italy is very different from the banking we simple English know of at home. Banking in England, like land-owning, has hitherto been a sort of hold up. There were always borrowers, there were always tenants, and all that had to be done was to refuse, obstruct, delay and worry the helpless borrower or would-be tenant until the maximum of security and profit was obtained. I have never borrowed but I have built, and I know something of the extreme hauteur of property of England towards a man who wants to do anything with land, and with money I gather the case is just the same. But in Italy, which already possessed a sunny prosperity of its own upon mediaeval lines, the banker has had to be suggestive and persuasive, sympathetic and helpful. These are unaccustomed attitudes for British capital. The field has been far more attractive to the German banker, who is less of a proudly impassive usurer and more of a partner, who demands less than absolute security because he investigates more industriously and intelligently. This great bank, the Banca Commerciale Italiana, is a bank of the German type: to begin with, it was certainly dominated by German directors; it was a bank of stimulation, and its activities interweave now into the whole fabric of Italian commercial life. But it has already liberated itself from German influence, and the bulk of its capital is Italian. Nevertheless I found discussion ranging about firstly what the Banca Commerciale essentially *was*, secondly what it might *become*, thirdly what it might *do*, and fourthly what, if anything, had to be done to it.

It is a novelty to an English mind to find banking thus mixed up with politics, but it is not a novelty in Italy. All over Venetia there are agricultural banks which are said to be "clerical." I grappled with this mystery. "How are they clerical?" I asked Captain Pirelli. "Do they lend money on bad security to clerical voters, and on no terms whatever to anti-clericals?" He was quite of my way of thinking. "*Pecunia non olet*," he said; "I have never yet smelt a clerical fifty lira note."... But on the other hand Italy is very close to Germany; she wants easy money for development, cheap coal, a market for various products. The case against the Germans—this case in which the Banca Commerciale Italiana appears, I am convinced unjustly, as a suspect—is that they have turned this natural and proper interchange with Italy into the acquisition of German power. That they have not been merely easy traders, but patriotic agents. It is alleged that they used their early "pull" in Italian banking to favour German enterprises and German political influence against the development of native Italian business; that their merchants are not bona-fide individuals, but members of a nationalist conspiracy to gain economic controls. The German is a patriotic monomaniac. He is not a man but a limb, the worshipper of a national effigy, the digit of an insanely proud and greedy Germania, and here are the natural consequences.

The case of the individual Italian compactly is this: "We do not like the Austrians and Germans. These Imperialisms look always over the Alps. Whatever increases German influence here threatens Italian life. The German is a German first and a human being afterwards.... But on the other hand England seems commercially indifferent to us and France has been economically hostile..."

"After all," I said presently, after reflection, "in that matter of *Pecunia non olet*; there used to be fusses about European loans in China. And one of the favourite themes of British fiction and drama before the war was the unfortunate position of the girl who accepted a loan from the wicked man to pay her debts at bridge."

"Italy," said Captain Pirelli, "isn't a girl. And she hasn't been playing bridge."

I incline on the whole to his point of view. Money is facile cosmopolitan stuff. I think that any bank that settles down in Italy is going to be slowly and steadily naturalised Italian, it will become more and more Italian until it is wholly Italian. I would trust Italy to make and keep the Banca Commerciale Italiana Italian. I believe the Italian brain is a better brain than the German article. But still I heard people talking of the implicated organisation as if it were engaged in the most insidious duplicities. "Wait for only a year or so after the war," said one English authority to me, "and the mask will be off and it will be frankly a 'Deutsche Bank' once more." They assure me that then German enterprises will be favoured again, Italian and Allied enterprises blockaded and embarrassed, the good understanding of Italians and English poisoned, entirely through this organisation....

The reasonable uncommercial man would like to reject all this last sort of talk as "suspicion mania." So far as the Banca Commerciale Italiana goes, I at least find that easy enough; I quote that instance simply because it is a case where suspicion has been dispelled, but in regard to a score of other business veins it is not so easy to dispel suspicion. This war has been a shock to reasonable men the whole world over. They have been forced to realise that after all a great number of Germans have been engaged in a crack-brained conspiracy against the non-German world; that in a great number of cases when one does business with a German the business does not end with the individual German. We hated to believe that a business could be tainted by German partners or German associations. If now we err on the side of over-suspicion, it is the German's little weakness for patriotic disingenuousness that is most to blame....

But anyhow I do not think there is much good in a kind of witch-smelling among Italian enterprises to find the hidden German. Certain things are necessary for Italian prosperity and Italy must get them. The Italians want intelligent and helpful capital. They want a helpful France. They want bituminous coal for metallurgical purposes. They want cheap shipping. The French too want metallurgical coal. It is more important for civilisation, for the general goodwill of the Allies and for Great Britain that these needs should be supplied than that individual British money-owners or ship-owners should remain sluggishly rich by insisting upon high security or high freights. The control of British coal-mining and shipping is in the national interests—for international interests—rather than for the creation of that particularly passive, obstructive, and wasteful type of wealth, the wealth of the mere profiteer, is as urgent a necessity for the commercial welfare of France and Italy and the endurance of the Great Alliance as it is for the well-being of the common man in Britain.

3

I left my military guide at Verona on Saturday afternoon and reached Milan in time to dine outside Salvini's in the Galleria Vittorio Emanuele, with an Italian fellow story-writer. The place was as full as ever; we had to wait for a table. It is notable that there were still great numbers of young men not in uniform in Milan and Turin and Vicenza and Verona; there was no effect anywhere of a depletion of men. The whole crowded place was smouldering with excitement. The diners looked about them as they talked, some talked loudly and seemed to be expressing sentiments. Newspaper vendors appeared at the intersection of the arcades, uttering ambiguous cries, and did a brisk business of flitting white sheets among the little tables.

"To-night," said my companion, "I think we shall declare war upon Germany. The decision is being made."

I asked intelligently why this had not been done before. I forget the precise explanation he gave. A young soldier in uniform, who had been dining at an adjacent table and whom I had not recognised before as a writer I had met some years previously in London, suddenly joined in our conversation, with a slightly different explanation. I had been carrying on a conversation in slightly ungainly French, but now I relapsed into English.

But indeed the matter of that declaration of war is as plain as daylight; the Italian national consciousness has not at first that direct sense of the German danger that exists in the minds of the three northern Allies. To the Italian the traditional enemy is Austria, and this war is not primarily a war for any other end than the emancipation of Italy. Moreover we have to remember that for years there has been serious commercial friction between France and Italy, and considerable mutual elbowing in North Africa. Both Frenchmen and Italians are resolute to remedy this now, but the restoration of really friendly and trustful relations is not to be done in a day. It has been an extraordinary misfortune for Great Britain that instead of boldly taking over her shipping from its private owners and using it all, regardless of their profit, in the interests of herself and her allies, her government has permitted so much of it as military and naval needs have not requisitioned to continue to ply for gain, which the government itself has shared by a tax on war profits. The Anglophobe elements in Italian public life have made the utmost of this folly or laxity in relation more particularly to the consequent dearness of coal in Italy. They have carried on an amazingly effective campaign in which this British slackness with the individual profiteer, is represented as if it were the deliberate greed of the British state. This certainly contributed very much to fortify Italy's disinclination to slam the door on the German connection.

I did my best to make it clear to my two friends that so far from England exploiting Italy, I myself suffered in exactly the same way as any Italian, through the extraordinary liberties of our shipping interest. "I pay as well as you do," I said; "the shippers' blockade of Great Britain is more effective than the submarines'. My food, my coal, my petrol are all restricted in the sacred name of private property. You see, capital in England has hitherto been not an exploitation but a hold-up. We are learning differently now.... And anyhow, Mr. Runciman has been here and given Italy assurances...."

In the train to Modane this old story recurred again. It is imperative that English readers should understand clearly how thoroughly these little matters have been *worked* by the enemy.

Some slight civilities led to a conversation that revealed the Italian lady in the corner as an Irishwoman married to an Italian, and also brought out the latent English of a very charming elderly lady opposite to her. She had heard a speech, a wonderful speech from a railway train, by "the Lord Runciman." He had said the most beautiful things about Italy.

I did my best to echo these beautiful things.

Then the Irishwoman remarked that Mr. Runciman had not satisfied everybody. She and her husband had met a minister—I found afterwards he was one of the members of the late Giolotti government—who had been talking very loudly and scornfully of the bargain Italy was making with England. I assured her that the desire of England was simply to give Italy all that she needed.

"But," said the husband casually, "Mr. Runciman is a shipowner."

I explained that he was nothing of the sort. It was true that he came of a shipowning family—and perhaps inherited a slight tendency to see things from a shipowning point of view—but in England we did not suspect a man on such a score as that.

"In Italy I think we should," said the husband of the Irish lady.

4

This incidental discussion is a necessary part of my impression of Italy at war. The two western allies and Great Britain in particular have to remember Italy's economic needs, and to prepare to rescue them from the blind exploitation of private profit. They have to remember these needs too, because, if they are left out of the picture, then it becomes impossible to understand the full measure of the risk Italy has faced in undertaking this war for an idea. With a Latin lucidity she has counted every risk, and with a Latin idealism she has taken her place by the side of those who fight for a liberal civilisation against a Byzantine imperialism.

As I came out of the brightly lit Galleria Vittorio Emanuele into the darkened Piazza del Duomo I stopped under the arcade and stood looking up at the shadowy darkness of that great pinnacled barn, that marble bride-cake, which is, I suppose, the last southward fortress of the Franco-English Gothic.

"It was here," said my host, "that we burnt the German stuff."

"What German stuff?"

"Pianos and all sorts of things. From the shops. It is possible, you know, to buy things too cheaply—and to give too much for the cheapness."

THE WESTERN WAR (SEPTEMBER, 1916)

I. RUINS

1

If I had to present some particular scene as typical of the peculiar vileness and mischief wrought by this modern warfare that Germany has elaborated and thrust upon the world, I do not think I should choose as my instance any of those great architectural wrecks that seem most to impress contemporary writers. I have seen the injuries and ruins of the cathedrals at Arras and Soissons and the wreckage of the great church at Saint Eloi, I have visited the Hotel de Ville at Arras and seen photographs of the present state of the Cloth Hall at Ypres—a building I knew very well indeed in its days of pride—and I have not been very deeply moved. I suppose that one is a little accustomed to Gothic ruins, and that there is always something monumental about old buildings; it is only a question of degree whether they are more or less tumble-down. I was far more desolated by the obliteration of such villages as Fricourt and Dompierre, and by the horrible state of the fields and gardens round about them, and my visit to Arras railway station gave me all the sensations of coming suddenly on a newly murdered body.

Before I visited the recaptured villages in the zone of the actual fighting, I had an idea that their evacuation was only temporary, that as soon as the war line moved towards Germany the people of the devastated villages would return to build their houses and till their fields again. But I see now that not only are homes and villages destroyed almost beyond recognition, but the very fields are destroyed. They are wildernesses of shell craters; the old worked soil is buried and great slabs of crude earth have been flung up over it. No ordinary plough will travel over this frozen sea, let along that everywhere chunks of timber, horrible tangles of rusting wire, jagged fragments of big shells, and a great number of unexploded shells are entangled in the mess. Often this chaos is stained bright yellow by high explosives, and across it run the twisting trenches and communication trenches eight, ten, or twelve feet deep. These will become water pits and mud pits into which beasts will fall. It is incredible that there should be crops from any of this region of the push for many years to come. There is no shade left; the roadside trees are splintered stumps with scarcely the spirit to put forth a leaf; a few stunted thistles and weeds are the sole proofs that life may still go on.

The villages of this wide battle region are not ruined; they are obliterated. It is just possible to trace the roads in them, because the roads have been cleared and repaired for the passing of the guns and ammunition. Fricourt is a tangle of German dug-outs. One dug-out in particular there promises to become a show place. It must be the masterpiece of some genius for dug-outs; it is made as if its makers enjoyed the job; it is like the work of some horrible badger among the vestiges of what were pleasant human homes. You are taken down a timbered staircase into its warren of rooms and passages; you are shown the places under the craters of the great British shells, where the wood splintered but did not come in. (But the arrival of those shells must have been a stunning moment.) There are a series of ingenious bolting shafts set with iron climbing bars. In this place German officers and soldiers have lived continually for nearly two years. This war is, indeed, a troglodytic propaganda. You come up at last at the far end into what was once a cellar of a decent Frenchman's home.

But there are stranger subterranean refuges than that at Fricourt. At Dompierre the German trenches skirted the cemetery, and they turned the dead out of their vaults and made lurking places of the tombs. I walked with M. Joseph Reinach about this place, picking our way carefully amidst the mud holes and the wire, and watched the shells bursting away over the receding battle line to the west. The wreckage of the graves was Durereqsue. And here would be a fragment of marble angle and here a split stone with an inscription. Splinters of coffins, rusty iron crosses and the petals of tin flowers were trampled into the mud, amidst the universal barbed wire. A little distance down the slope is a brand new cemetery, with new metal wreaths and even a few flowers; it is a disciplined array of uniform wooden crosses, each with its list of soldiers' names. Unless I am wholly mistaken in France no Germans will ever get a chance for ever more to desecrate that second cemetery as they have done its predecessor.

We walked over the mud heaps and litter that had once been houses towards the centre of Dompierre village, and tried to picture to ourselves what the place had been. Many things are recognisable in Dompierre that have altogether vanished at Fricourt; for instance, there are quire large triangular pieces of the church wall upstanding at Dompierre. And a mile away perhaps down the hill on the road towards Amiens, the ruins of the sugar refinery are very distinct. A sugar refinery is an affair of big iron receptacles and great flues and pipes and so forth, and iron does not go down under gun fire as stone or brick does. The whole fabric wars rust, bent and twisted, gaping with shell holes, that raggedest display of old iron, but it still kept its general shape, as a smashed, battered, and sunken ironclad might do at the bottom of the sea.

There wasn't a dog left of the former life of Dompierre. There was not even much war traffic that morning on the worn and muddy road. The guns muttered some miles away to the west, and a lark sang. But a little way farther on up the road was an intermediate dressing station, rigged up with wood and tarpaulins, and orderlies were packing two wounded men into an ambulance. The men on the stretchers were grey faced, as though they had been trodden on by some gigantic dirty boot.

As we came back towards where our car waited by the cemetery I heard the jingle of a horseman coming across the space behind us. I turned and beheld one of the odd contrasts that seem always to be happening in this incredible war. This man was, I suppose, a native officer of some cavalry force from French north Africa. He was a handsome dark brown Arab, wearing a long yellow-white robe and a tall cap about which ran a band of sheepskin. He was riding one of those little fine lean horses with long tails that I think are Barbary horses, his archaic saddle rose fore and aft of him, and the turned-up toes of his soft leather boots were stuck into great silver stirrups. He might have ridden straight out of the Arabian nights. He passed thoughtfully, picking his way delicately among the wire and the shell craters, and coming into the road, broke into a canter and vanished in the direction of the smashed-up refinery.

2

About such towns as Rheims or Arras or Soissons there is an effect of waiting stillness like nothing else I have ever experienced. At Arras the situation is almost incredible to the civilian mind. The British hold the town, the Germans hold a northern suburb; at one point near the river the trenches are just four metres apart. This state of tension has lasted for long months.

Unless a very big attack is contemplated, I suppose there is no advantage in an assault; across that narrow interval we should only get into trenches that might be costly or impossible to hold, and so it would be for the Germans on our side. But there is a kind of etiquette observed; loud vulgar talking on either side of the four-metre gap leads at once to bomb throwing. And meanwhile on both sides guns of various calibre keep up an intermittent fire, the German guns register—I think that is the right term—on the cross of Arras cathedral, the British guns search lovingly for the German batteries. As one walks about the silent streets one hears, "*Bang*—Pheeee—woooo" and then far away "*dump*." One of ours. Then presently back comes "Pheeee—woooo—*Bang!*" One of theirs.

Amidst these pleasantries, the life of the town goes on. *Le Lion d'Arras*, an excellent illustrated paper, produces its valiant sheets, and has done so since the siege began.

The current number of *Le Lion d'Arras* had to report a local German success. Overnight they had killed a gendarme. There is to be a public funeral and much ceremony. It is rare for anyone now to get killed; everything is so systematised.

You may buy postcards with views of the destruction at various angles, and send them off with the Arras postmark. The town is not without a certain business activity. There is, I am told, a considerable influx of visitors of a special sort; they wear khaki and lead the troglodytic life. They play cards and gossip and sleep in the shadows, and may not walk the streets. I had one glimpse of a dark crowded cellar. Now and then one sees a British soldier on some special errand; he keeps to the pavement, mindful of the spying German sausage balloon in the air. The streets are strangely quite and grass grows between the stones.

The Hotel de Ville and the cathedral are now mostly heaps of litter, but many streets of the town have suffered very little. Here and there a house has been crushed and one or two have been bisected, the front reduced to a heap of splinters and the back halves of the rooms left so that one sees the bed, the hanging end of the carpet, the clothes cupboard yawning open, the pictures still on the wall. In one place a lamp stands on a chest of drawers, on a shelf of floor cut off completely from the world below.... Pheeee—woooo—*Bang!* One would be irresistibly reminded of a Sunday afternoon in the city of London, if it were not for those unmeaning explosions.

I went to the station, a dead railway station. A notice-board requested us to walk around the silent square on the outside pavement and not across it. The German sausage balloon had not been up for days; it had probably gone off to the Somme; the Somme was a terrible vortex just then which was sucking away the resources of the whole German line; but still discipline is discipline. The sausage might come peeping up at any moment over the station roof, and so we skirted the square. Arras was fought for in the early stages of the war; two lines of sand-bagged breastworks still run obliquely through the station; one is where the porters used to put luggage upon cabs and one runs the length of the platform. The station was a fine one of the modern type, with a glass roof whose framework still remains, though the glass powders the floor and is like a fine angular gravel underfoot. The rails are rails of rust, and cornflowers and mustard and tall grasses grow amidst the ballast. The waiting-rooms have suffered from a shell or so, but there are still the sofas of green plush, askew, a little advertisement hung from the wall, the glass smashed. The ticket bureau is as if a giant had scattered a great number of tickets, mostly still done up in bundles, to Douai, to Valenciennes, to Lens and so on. These tickets are souvenirs too portable to resist. I gave way to that common weakness.

I went out and looked up and down the line; two deserted goods trucks stood as if they sheltered under a footbridge. The grass poked out through their wheels. The railway signals seemed uncertain in their intimations; some were up and some were down. And it was as still and empty as a summer afternoon in Pompeii. No train has come into Arras for two long years now.

We lunched in a sunny garden with various men who love Arras but are weary of it, and we disputed about Irish politics. We discussed the political future of Sir F. E. Smith. We also disputed whether there was an equivalent in English for *embusque*. Every now and then a shell came over—an aimless shell.

A certain liveliness marked our departure from the town. Possibly the Germans also listen for the rare infrequent automobile. At any rate, as we were just starting our way back—it is improper to mention the exact point from which we started—came "Pheeee—-woooo." Quite close. But there was no *Bang!* One's mind hung expectant and disappointed. It was a dud shell.

And then suddenly I became acutely aware of the personality of our chauffeur. It was not his business to talk to us, but he turned his head, showed a sharp profile, wry lips and a bright excited eye, and remarked, "*That* was a near one—anyhow." He then cut a corner over the pavement and very nearly cut it through a house. He bumped us over a shell hole and began to toot his horn. At every gateway, alley, and cross road on this silent and empty streets of Arras and frequently in between, he tooted punctiliously. (It is not proper to sound motor horns in Arras.) I cannot imagine what the listening Germans made of it. We passed the old gates of that city of fear, still tooting vehemently, and then with shoulders eloquent of his feelings, our chauffeur abandoned the horn altogether and put his whole soul into the accelerator....

3

Soissons was in very much the same case as Arras. There was the same pregnant silence in her streets, the same effect of waiting for the moment which draws nearer and nearer, when the brooding German lines away there will be full of the covert activities of retreat, when the streets of the old town will stir with the joyous excitement of the conclusive advance.

The organisation of Soissons for defence is perfect. I may not describe it, but think of whatever would stop and destroy an attacking party or foil the hostile shell. It is there. Men have had nothing else to do and nothing else to think of for two years. I crossed the bridge the English made in the pursuit after the Marne, and went into the first line trenches and peeped towards the invisible enemy. To show me exactly where to look a seventy-five obliged with a shell. In the crypt of the Abbey of St. Medard near by it—it must provoke the Germans bitterly to think that all the rest of the building vanished ages ago—the French boys sleep beside the bones of King Childebert the Second. They shelter safely in the prison of Louis the Pious. An ineffective shell from a German seventy-seven burst in the walled garden close at hand as I came out from those thousand-year-old memories again.

The cathedral at Soissons had not been nearly so completely smashed up as the one at Arras; I doubt if it has been very greatly fired into. There is a peculiar beauty in the one long vertical strip of blue sky between the broken arches in the chief gap where the wall has tumbled in. And the people are holding on in many cases exactly as they are doing in Arras; I do not know whether it is habit or courage that is most apparent in this persistence. About the chief place of the town there are ruined houses, but some invisible hand still keeps the grass of the little garden within bounds and has put out a bed of begonias. In Paris I met a charming American writer, the wife of a French artist, the lady who wrote *My House on the Field of Honour*. She gave me a queer little anecdote. On account of some hospital work she had been allowed to visit Soissons—a rare privilege for a woman—and she stayed the night in a lodging. The room into which she was shown was like any other French provincial bedroom, and after her Anglo-Saxon habit she walked straight to the windows to open them.

They looked exactly like any other French bedroom windows, with neat, clean white lace curtains across them. The curtains had been put there, because they were the proper things to put there.

"Madame," said the hostess, "need not trouble to open the glass. There is no more glass in Soissons."

But there were curtains nevertheless. There was all the precise delicacy of the neatly curtained home life of France.

And she told me too of the people at dinner, and how as the little serving-maid passed about a proud erection of cake and conserve and cream, came the familiar "Pheeee—-woooo—*Bang!*"

"That must have been the Seminaire," said someone.

As one speaks of the weather or a passing cart.

"It was in the Rue de la Bueire, M'sieur," the little maid asserted with quiet conviction, poising the trophy of confectionery for Madame Huard with an unshaking hand.

So stoutly do the roots of French life hold beneath the tramplings of war.

II. THE GRADES OF WAR

1 Soissons and Arras when I visited them were samples of the deadlock war; they were like Bloch come true. The living fact about war so far is that Bloch has not come true—*yet*. I think in the end he will come true, but not so far as this war is concerned, and to make that clear it is necessary to trouble the reader with a little disquisition upon war—omitting as far as humanly possible all mention of Napoleon's campaigns.

The development of war has depended largely upon two factors. One of these is invention. New weapons and new methods have become available, and have modified tactics, strategy, the relative advantage of offensive and defensive. The other chief factor in the evolution of the war has been social organisation. As Machiavelli points out in his *Art of War*, there was insufficient social stability in Europe to keep a properly trained and disciplined infantry in the field from the passing of the Roman legions to the appearance of the Swiss footmen. He makes it very clear that he considers the fighting of the Middle Ages, though frequent and bloody, to be a confused, mobbing sort of affair, and politically and technically unsatisfactory. The knight was an egotist in armour. Machiavelli does small justice to the English bowmen. It is interesting to note that Switzerland, that present island of peace, was regarded by him as the mother of modern war. Swiss aggression was the curse of the Milanese. That is a remark by the way; our interest here is to note that modern war emerges upon history as the sixteenth century unfolds, as an affair in which the essential factor is the drilled and trained infantryman. The artillery is developing as a means of breaking the infantry; cavalry for charging them when broken, for pursuit and scouting. To this day this triple division of forces dominates soldiers' minds. The mechanical development of warfare has consisted largely in the development of facilities for enabling or hindering the infantry to get to close quarters. As that has been made easy or difficult the offensive or the defensive has predominated.

A history of military method for the last few centuries would be a record of successive alternate steps in which offensive and defensive contrivances pull ahead, first one and then the other. Their relative fluctuations are marked by the varying length of campaigns. From the very outset we have the ditch and the wall; the fortified place upon a pass or main road, as a check to the advance. Artillery improves, then fortification improves. The defensive holds its own for a long period, wars are mainly siege wars, and for a century before the advent of Napoleon there are no big successful sweeping invasions, no marches upon the enemy capital and so on. There were wars of reduction, wars of annoyance. Napoleon developed the offensive by seizing upon the enthusiastic infantry of the republic, improving transport and mobile artillery, using road-making as an aggressive method. In spite of the successful experiment of Torres Vedras and the warning of Plevna the offensive remained dominant throughout the nineteenth century.

But three things were working quietly towards the rehabilitation of the defensive; firstly the increased range, accuracy and rapidity of rifle fire, with which we may include the development of the machine gun; secondly the increasing use of the spade, and thirdly the invention of barbed wire. By the end of the century these things had come so far into military theory as to produce the great essay of Bloch, and to surprise the British military people, who are not accustomed to read books or talk shop, in the Boer war. In the thinly populated war region of South Africa the difficulties of forcing entrenched positions were largely met by outflanking, the Boers had only a limited amount of barbed wire and could be held down in their trenches by shrapnel, and even at the beginning of the present war there can be little doubt that we and our Allies were still largely unprepared for the full possibilities of trench warfare, we attempted a war of manoeuvres, war at about the grade to which war had been brought in 1898, and it was the Germans who first brought the war up to date by entrenching upon the Aisne. We had, of course, a few aeroplanes at that time, but they were used chiefly as a sort of accessory cavalry for scouting; our artillery was light and our shell almost wholly shrapnel.

Now the grades of warfare that have been developed since the present war began, may be regarded as a series of elaborations and counter elaborations of the problem which begins as a line of trenches behind wire, containing infantry with rifles and machine guns. Against this an infantry attack with bayonet, after shrapnel fails. This we will call Grade A. To this the offensive replies with improved artillery, and particularly with high explosive shell instead of shrapnel. By this the wire is blown away, the trench wrecked and the defender held down as the attack charges up. This is Grade B. But now appear the dug-out elaborating the trench and the defensive battery behind the trench. The defenders, under the preliminary bombardment, get into the dug-outs with their rifles and machine guns, and emerge as fresh as paint as the attack comes up. Obviously there is much scope for invention and contrivance in the dug-out as the reservoir of counter attacks. Its possibilities have been very ably exploited by the Germans. Also the defensive batteries behind, which have of course the exact range of the captured trench, concentrate on it and destroy the attack at the moment of victory. The trench falls back to its former holders under this fire and a counter attack. Check again for the offensive. Even if it can take, it cannot hold a position under these conditions. This we will call Grade A2; a revised and improved A. What is the retort from the opposite side? Obviously to enhance and extend the range of the preliminary bombardment behind the actual trench line, to destroy or block, if it can, the dug-outs and destroy or silence the counter offensive artillery. If it can do that, it can go on; otherwise Bloch wins.

If fighting went on only at ground level Bloch would win at this stage, but here it is that the aeroplane comes in. From the ground it would be practically impossible to locate the enemies' dug-outs, secondary defences, and batteries. But the aeroplane takes us immediately into a new grade of warfare, in which the location of the defender's secondary trenches, guns, and even machine-gun positions becomes a matter of extreme precision—provided only that the offensive has secured command of the air and can send his aeroplanes freely over the defender lines. Then the preliminary bombardment becomes of a much more extensive character; the defender's batteries are tackled by the overpowering fire of guns they are unable to locate and answer; the secondary dug-outs and strong places are plastered down, a barrage fire shuts off support from the doomed trenches, the men in these trenches are held down by a concentrated artillery fire and the attack goes up at last to hunt them out of the dug-outs and collect the survivors. Until the attack is comfortably established in the captured trench, the fire upon the old counter attack position goes on. This is the grade, Grade B2, to which modern warfare has attained upon the Somme front. The appearance of the Tank has only increased the offensive advantage. There at present warfare rests.

There is, I believe, only one grade higher possible. The success of B2 depends upon the completeness of the aerial observation. The invention of an anti-aircraft gun which would be practically sure of hitting and bringing down an aeroplane at any height whatever up to 20,000 feet, would restore the defensive and establish what I should think must be the final grade of war, A3. But at present nothing of the sort exists and nothing of the sort is likely to exist for a very long time; at present hitting an aeroplane by any sort of gun at all is a rare and uncertain achievement. Such a gun is not impossible and therefore we must suppose such a gun will some day be constructed, but it will be of a novel type and character, unlike anything at present in existence. The grade of fighting that I was privileged to witness on the Somme, the grade at which a steady successful offensive is possible, is therefore, I conclude, the grade at which the present war will end.

2

But now having thus spread out the broad theory of the business, let me go on to tell some of the actualities of the Somme offensive. They key fact upon both British and French fronts was the complete ascendancy of the Allies aeroplanes. It is the necessary preliminary condition for the method upon which the great generals of the French army rely in this sanitary task of shoving the German Thing off the soil of Belgium and France back into its own land. A man who is frequently throwing out prophecies is bound to score a few successes, and one that I may legitimately claim is my early insistence upon that fact that the equality of the German aviator was likely to be inferior to that of his French or British rival. The ordinary German has neither the flexible quality of body, the quickness of nerve, the temperament, nor the mental habits that make a successful aviator. This idea was first put into my head by considering the way in which Germans walk and carry themselves, and by nothing the difference in nimbleness between the cyclists in the streets of German and French towns. It was confirmed by a conversation I had with a German aviator who was also a dramatist, and who came to see me upon some copyright matter in 1912. He broached the view that aviation would destroy democracy, because he said only aristocrats make aviators. (He was a man of good family.) With a duke or so in my mind I asked him why. Because, he explained, a man without aristocratic quality in tradition, cannot possibly endure the "high loneliness" of the air. That sounded rather like nonsense at the time, and then I reflected that for a Prussian that might be true. There may be something in the German composition that does demand association and the support of pride and training before dangers can be faced. The Germans are social and methodical, the French and English are by comparison chaotic and instinctive; perhaps the very readiness for a conscious orderliness that makes the German so formidable upon the ground, so thorough and fore-seeking, makes him slow and unsure in the air. At any rate the experiences of this war have seemed to carry out this hypothesis. The German aviators will not as a class stand up to those of the Allies. They are not nimble in the air. Such champions as they have produced have been men of one trick; one of their great men, Immelmann—he was put down by an English boy a month or so ago—had a sort of hawk's swoop. He would go very high and then come down at his utmost pace at his antagonist, firing his machine gun at him as he came. If he missed in this hysterical lunge, he went on down.... This does not strike the Allied aviator as very brilliant. A gentleman of that sort can sooner or later be caught on the rise by going for him over the German lines.

The first phase, then, of the highest grade offensive, the ultimate development of war regardless of expense, is the clearance of the air. Such German machines as are up are put down by fighting aviators. These last fly high; in the clear blue of the early morning they look exactly like gnats; some trail a little smoke in the sunshine; they take their machine guns in pursuit over the German lines, and the German anti-aircraft guns, the

Archibalds, begin to pattern the sky about them with little balls of black smoke. From below one does not see men nor feel that men are there; it is as if it were an affair of midges. Close after the fighting machines come the photographic aeroplanes, with cameras as long as a man is high, flying low—at four or five thousand feet that is—over the enemy trenches. The Archibald leaves these latter alone; it cannot fire a shell to explode safely so soon after firing; but they are shot at with rifles and machine guns. They do not mind being shot at; only the petrol tank and the head and thorax of the pilot are to be considered vital. They will come back with forty or fifty bullet holes in the fabric. They will go under this fire along the length of the German positions exposing plate after plate; one machine will get a continuous panorama of many miles and then come back straight to the aerodrome to develop its plates.

There is no waste of time about the business, the photographs are developed as rapidly as possible. Within an hour and a half after the photographs were taken the first prints are going back into the bureau for the examination of the photographs. Both British and French air photographs are thoroughly scrutinised and marked.

An air photograph to an inexperienced eye is not a very illuminating thing; one makes our roads, blurs of wood, and rather vague buildings. But the examiner has an eye that has been in training; he is a picked man; he has at hand yesterday's photographs and last week's photographs, marked maps and all sorts of aids and records. If he is a Frenchman he is only too happy to explain his ideas and methods. Here, he will point out, is a little difference between the German trench beyond the wood since yesterday. For a number of reasons he thinks that will be a new machine gun emplacement; here at the centre of the farm wall they have been making another. This battery here—isn't it plain? Well, it's a dummy. The grass in front of it hasn't been scorched, and there's been no serious wear on the road here for a week. Presently the Germans will send one or two waggons up and down that road and instruct them to make figures of eight to imitate scorching on the grass in front of the gun. We know all about that. The real wear on the road, compare this and this and this, ends here at this spot. It turns off into the wood. There's a sort of track in the trees. Now look where the trees are just a little displaced! (This lens is rather better for that.) *That's* one gun. You see? Here, I will show you another....

That process goes on two or three miles behind the front line. Very clean young men in white overalls do it as if it were a labour of love. And the Germans in the trenches, the German gunners, *know it is going on.* They know that in the quickest possible way these observations of the aeroplane that was over them just now will go to the gunners. The careful gunner, firing by the map and marking by aeroplane, kite balloon or direct observation, will be getting onto the located guns and machine guns in another couple of hours. The French claim that they have located new batteries, got their *tir de demolition* upon them in and destroyed them within five hours. The British I told of that found it incredible. Every day the French print special maps showing the guns, sham guns, trenches, everything of significance behind the German lines, showing everything that has happened in the last four-and-twenty hours. It is pitiless. It is indecent. The map-making and printing goes on in the room next and most convenient to the examination of the photographs. And, as I say, the German army knows of this, and knows that it cannot prevent it because of its aerial weakness. That knowledge is not the last among the forces that is crumpling up the German resistance upon the Somme.

I visited some French guns during the *tir de demolition* phase. I counted nine aeroplanes and twenty-six kite balloons in the air at the same time. There was nothing German visible in the air at all.

It is a case of eyes and no eyes.

The French attack resolves itself into a triple system of gunfire. First for a day or so, or two or three days, there is demolition fire to smash up all the exactly located batteries, organisation, supports, behind the front line enemy trenches; then comes barrage fire to cut off supplies and reinforcements; then, before the advance, the hammering down fire, "heads down," upon the trenches. When at last this stops and the infantry goes forward to rout out the trenches and the dug-outs, they go forward with a minimum of inconvenience. The first wave of attack fights, destroys, or disarms the surviving Germans and sends them back across the open to the French trenches. They run as fast as they can, hands up, and are shepherded farther back. The French set to work to turn over the captured trenches and organise themselves against any counter attack that may face the barrage fire.

That is the formula of the present fighting, which the French have developed. After an advance there is a pause, while the guns move up nearer the Germans and fresh aeroplane reconnaissance goes on. Nowhere on this present offensive has a German counter attack had more than the most incidental success; and commonly they have had frightful losses. Then after a few days of refreshment and accumulation, the Allied attack resumes.

That is the perfected method of the French offensive. I had the pleasure of learning its broad outlines in good company, in the company of M. Joseph Reinach and Colonel Carence, the military writer. Their talk together and with me in the various messes at which we lunched was for the most part a keen discussion of every detail and every possibility of the offensive machine; every French officer's mess seems a little council upon the one supreme question in France, *how to do it best*. M. Reinach has made certain suggestions about the co-operation of the French and British that I will discuss elsewhere, but one great theme was the constitution of "the ideal battery." For years French military thought has been acutely attentive to the best number of guns for effective common action, and has tended rather to the small battery theory. My two companies were playing with the idea that the ideal battery was a battery of one big gun, with its own aeroplane and kite balloon marking for it.

The British seem to be associated with the adventurous self-reliance needed in the air. The British aeroplanes do not simply fight the Germans out of the sky; they also make themselves an abominable nuisance by bombing the enemy trenches. For every German bomb that is dropped by aeroplane on or behind the British lines, about twenty go down on the heads of the Germans. British air bombs upon guns, stores and communications do some of the work that the French effect by their systematic demolition fire.

And the British aviator has discovered and is rapidly developing an altogether fresh branch of air activity in the machine-gun attack at a very low altitude. Originally I believe this was tried in western Egypt, but now it is being increasingly used upon the British front in France. An aeroplane which comes down suddenly, travelling very rapidly, to a few hundred feet, is quite hard to hit, even if it is not squirting bullets from a machine gun as it advances. Against infantry in the open this sort of thing is extremely demoralising. It is a method of attack still in its infancy, but there are great possibilities for it in the future, when the bending and cracking German line gives, as ultimately it must give if this offensive does not relax. If the Allies persist in their pressure upon the western front, if there is no relaxation in the supply of munitions from Britain and no lapse into tactical stupidity, a German retreat eastward is inevitable.

Now a cavalry pursuit alone may easily come upon disaster, cavalry can be so easily held up by wire and a few machine guns. I think the Germans have reckoned on that and on automobiles, probably only the decay of their *morale* prevents their opening their lines now on the chance of the British attempting some such folly as a big cavalry advance, but I do not think the Germans have reckoned on the use of machine guns in aeroplanes, supported by and supporting cavalry or automobiles. At the present time I should imagine there is no more perplexing consideration amidst the many perplexities of the German military intelligence than the new complexion put upon pursuit by these low level air developments. It may mean that in all sorts of positions where they had counted confidently on getting away, they may not be able to get away—from the face of a scientific advance properly commanding and using modern material in a dexterous and intelligent manner.

III. THE WAR LANDSCAPE

1

I saw rather more of the British than of the French aviators because of the vileness of the weather when I visited the latter. It is quite impossible for me to institute comparisons between these two services. I should think that the British organisation I saw would be hard to beat, and that none but the French could hope to beat it. On the Western front the aviation has been screwed up to a very much higher level than on the Italian line. In Italy it has not become, as it has in France, the decisive factor. The war on the Carso front in Italy—I say nothing of the mountain warfare, which is a thing in itself—is in fact still in the stage that I have called B. It is good warfare well waged, but not such an intensity of warfare. It has not, as one says of pianos and voices, the same compass.

This is true in spite of the fact that the Italians along of all the western powers have adopted a type of aeroplane larger and much more powerful than anything except the big Russian machines. They are not at all suitable for any present purpose upon the Italian front, but at a later stage, when the German is retiring and Archibald no longer searches the air, they would be invaluable on the western front because of their enormous bomb or machine gun carrying capacity. "But sufficient for the day is the swat thereof," as the British public schoolboy says, and no doubt we shall get them when we have sufficiently felt the need for them. The big Caproni machines which the Italians possess are of 300 h.p. and will presently be of 500 h.p. One gets up a gangway into them was one gets into a yacht; they wave a main deck, a forward machine gun deck and an aft machine gun; one may walk about in them; in addition to guns and men they carry a very considerable weight of bombs beneath. They cannot of course beget up with the speed nor soar to the height of our smaller aeroplanes; it is as carriers in raids behind a force of fighting machines that they should find their use.

The British establishment I visited was a very refreshing and reassuring piece of practical organisation. The air force of Great Britain has had the good fortune to develop with considerable freedom from old army tradition; many of its officers are ex-civil engineers and so forth; Headquarters is a little shy of technical direction; and all this in a service that is still necessarily experimental and plastic is to the good. There is little doubt that, given a release from prejudice, bad associations and the equestrian tradition, British technical intelligence and energy can do just as well as the French. Our problem with our army is not to create intelligence, there is an abundance of it, but to release it from a dreary social and official pressure. The air service ransacks the army for men with technical training and sees that it gets them, there is a real keenness upon the work, and the men in these great mobile hangars talk shop readily and clearly.

I have already mentioned and the newspapers have told abundantly of the pluck, daring, and admirable work of our aviators; what is still untellable in any detail is the energy and ability of the constructive and repairing branch upon whose efficiency their feats depend. Perhaps the most interesting thing I saw in connection with the air work was the hospital for damaged machines and the dump to which those hopelessly injured are taken, in order that they may be disarticulated and all that is sound in them used for reconstruction. How excellently this work is being done may be judged from the fact that our offensive in July started with a certain number of aeroplanes, a number that would have seemed fantastic in a story a year before the war began. These aeroplanes were in constant action; they fought, they were shot down, they had their share of accidents. Not only did the repair department make good every loss, but after three weeks of the offensive the army was fighting with fifty more machines than at the outset. One goes through a vast Rembrandtesque shed opening upon a great sunny field, in whose cool shadows rest a number of interesting patients; captured and slightly damaged German machines, machines of our own with scars of battle upon them, one or two cases of bad landing. The star case came over from Peronne. It had come in two days ago.

I examined this machine and I will tell the state it was in, but I perceive that what I have to tell will read not like a sober statement of truth but like strained and silly lying. The machine had had a direct hit from an Archibald shell. The propeller had been clean blown away; so had the machine gun and all its fittings. The engines had been stripped naked and a good deal bent about. The timber stay over the aviator had been broken, so that it is marvellous the wings of the machine did not just up at once like the wings of a butterfly. The solitary aviator had been wounded in the face. He had then come down in a long glide into the British lines, and made a tolerable landing....

2

One consequence of the growing importance of the aeroplane in warfare is the development of a new military art, the art of camouflage. Camouflage is humbugging disguise, it is making things—and especially in this connection, military things—seem not what they are, but something peaceful and rural, something harmless and quite uninteresting to aeroplane observers. It is the art of making big guns look like haystacks and tents like level patches of field.

Also it includes the art of making attractive models of guns, camps, trenches and the like that are not bona-fide guns, camps, or trenches at all, so that the aeroplane bomb-dropper and the aeroplane observer may waste his time and energies and the enemy gunfire be misdirected. In Italy I saw dummy guns so made as to deceive the very elect at a distance of a few thousand feet. The camouflage of concealment aims either at invisibility or imitation; I have seen a supply train look like a row of cottages, its smoke-stack a chimney, with the tops of sham palings running along the back of the engine and creepers painted up its sides. But that was a flight of the imagination; the commonest camouflage is merely to conceal. Trees are brought up and planted near the object to be hidden, it is painted in the same tones as its background, it is covered with an awning painted to look like grass or earth. I suppose it is only a matter of development before a dummy cow or so is put up to chew the cud on the awning.

But camouflage or no camouflage, the bulk of both the French and British forces in the new won ground of the great offensive lay necessarily in the open. Only the big guns and the advanced Red Cross stations had got into pits and subterranean hiding places. The advance has been too rapid and continuous for the armies to make much of a toilette as they halted, and the destruction and the desolation of the country won afforded few facilities for easy concealment. Tents, transport, munitions, these all indicated an army on the march—at the rate of half a mile in a week or so, to Germany. If the wet and mud of November and December have for a time delayed that advance, the force behind has but accumulated for the resumption of the thrust.

3

A journey up from the base to the front trenches shows an interesting series of phases. One leaves Amiens, in which the normal life threads its way through crowds of resting men in khaki and horizon blue, in which staff officers in automobiles whisk hither and thither, in which there are nurses and even a few inexplicable ladies in worldly costume, in which restaurants and cafes are congested and busy, through which there is a perpetual coming and going of processions of heavy vans to the railway sidings. One dodges past a monstrous blue-black gun going up to the British front behind two resolute traction engines—the three sun-blistered young men in the cart that trails behind lounge in attitudes of haughty pride that would shame the ceiling gods of Hampton Court. One passes through arcades of waiting motor vans, through arcades of waiting motor vans, through suburbs still more intensely khaki or horizon blue, and so out upon the great straight poplar-edged road—to the front. Sometimes one laces through spates of heavy traffic, sometimes the dusty road is clear ahead, now we pass a vast aviation camp, now a park of waiting field guns, now an encampment of cavalry. One turns aside, and abruptly one is in France—France as one knew it before the war, on a shady secondary road, past a delightful chateau behind its iron gates, past a beautiful church, and then suddenly we are in a village street full of stately Indian soldiers.

It betrays no military secret to say that commonly the rare tourist to the British offensive passes through Albert, with its great modern red cathedral smashed to pieces and the great gilt Madonna and Child that once surmounted the tower now, as everyone knows, hanging out horizontally in an attitude that irresistibly suggests an imminent dive upon the passing traveller. One looks right up under it.

Presently we begin to see German prisoners. The whole lot look entirely contented, and are guarded by perhaps a couple of men in khaki. These German prisoners do not attempt to escape, they have not the slightest desire for any more fighting, they have done their bit, they say, honour is satisfied; they give remarkably little trouble. A little way further on perhaps we pass their cage, a double barbed-wire enclosure with a few tents and huts within.

A string of covered waggons passes by. I turn and see a number of men sitting inside and looking almost as cheerful as a beanfeast in Epping Forest. They make facetious gestures. They have a subdued sing-song going on. But one of them looks a little sick, and then I notice not very obtrusive bandages. "Sitting-up cases," my guide explains.

These are part of the casualties of last night's fight.

The fields on either side are now more evidently in the war zone. The array of carts, the patches of tents, the coming and going of men increases. But here are three women harvesting, and presently in a cornfield are German prisoners working under one old Frenchman. Then the fields become trampled again. Here is a village, not so very much knocked about, and passing through it we go slowly beside a long column of men going up to the front. We scan their collars for signs of some familiar regiment. These are new men going up for the first time; there is a sort of solemn elation in many of their faces.

The men coming down are usually smothered in mud or dust, and unless there has been a fight they look pretty well done up. They stoop under their equipment, and some of the youngsters drag. One pleasant thing about this coming down is the welcome of the regimental band, which is usually at work as soon as the men turn off from the high road. I hear several bands on the British front; they do much to enhance the general cheerfulness. On one of these days of my tour I had the pleasure of seeing the ——th Blankshires coming down after a fight. As we drew near I saw that they combined an extreme muddiness with an unusual elasticity. They all seemed to be looking us in the face instead of being too fagged to bother. Then I noticed a nice grey helmet dangling from one youngster's bayonet, in fact his eye directed me to it. A man behind him had a black German helmet of the type best known in English illustrations; then two more grey appeared. The catch of helmets was indeed quite considerable. Then I perceived on the road bank above and marching parallel with this column, a double file of still muddier Germans. Either they wore caps or went bare-headed. There were no helmets among them. We do not rob our prisoners but—a helmet is a weapon. Anyhow, it is an irresistible souvenir.

Now and then one sees afar off an ammunition dump, many hundreds of stacks of shells—without their detonators as yet—being unloaded from railway trucks, transferred from the broad gauge to the narrow gauge line, or loaded onto motor trolleys. Now and then one crosses a railway line. The railway lines run everywhere behind the British front, the construction follows the advance day by day. They go up as fast as the guns. One's guide remarks as the car bumps over the level crossing, "That is one of Haig's railways." It is an aspect of the Commander-in-Chief that has much impressed and pleased the men. And at last we begin to enter the region of the former Allied trenches, we pass the old German front line, we pass ruined houses, ruined fields, and thick patches of clustering wooden crosses and boards where the dead of the opening assaults lie. There are no more reapers now, there is no more green upon the fields, there is no green anywhere, scarcely a tree survives by the roadside, but only overthrown trunks and splintered stumps; the fields are wildernesses of shell craters and coarse weeds, the very woods are collections of blasted stems and stripped branches. This absolutely ravaged and ruined battlefield country extends now along the front of the Somme offensive for a depth of many miles; across it the French and British camps and batteries creep forward, the stores, the dumps, the railways creep forward, in their untiring, victorious thrust against the German lines. Overhead hum and roar the aeroplanes, away towards the enemy the humped, blue sausage-shaped kite balloons brood thoughtfully, and from this point and that, guns, curiously invisible until they speak, flash suddenly and strike their one short hammer-blow of sound.

Then one sees an enemy shell drop among the little patch of trees on the crest to the right, and kick up a great red-black mass of smoke and dust. We see it, and then we hear the whine of its arrival and at last the bang. The

Germans are blind now, they have lost the air, they are firing by guesswork and their knowledge of the abandoned territory.

"They think they have got divisional headquarters there," someone remarks.... "They haven't. But they keep on."

In this zone where shells burst the wise automobile stops and tucks itself away as inconspicuously as possible close up to a heap of ruins. There is very little traffic on the road now except for a van or so that hurries up, unloads, and gets back as soon as possible. Mules and men are taking the stuff the rest of the journey. We are in a flattened village, all undermined by dug-outs that were in the original German second line. We report ourselves to a young troglodyte in one of these, and are given a guide, and so set out on the last part of the journey to the ultimate point, across the land of shell craters and barbed wire litter and old and new trenches. We have all put on British steel helmets, hard but heavy and inelegant head coverings. I can write little that is printable about these aesthetic crimes. The French and German helmets are noble and beautiful things. These lumpish *pans*...

They ought to be called by the name of the man who designed them.

Presently we are advised to get into a communication trench. It is not a very attractive communication trench, and we stick to our track across the open. Three or four shells shiver overhead, but we decide they are British shells, going out. We reach a supporting trench in which men are waiting in a state of nearly insupportable boredom for the midday stew, the one event of interest in a day-long vigil. Here we are told imperatively to come right in at once, and we do.

All communication trenches are tortuous and practically endless. On an offensive front they have vertical sides of unsupported earth and occasional soakaways for rain, covered by wooden gratings, and they go on and on and on. At rare intervals they branch, and a notice board says "To Regent Street," or "To Oxford Street," or some such lie. It is all just trench. For a time you talk, but talking in single file soon palls. You cease to talk, and trudge. A great number of telephone wires come into the trench and cross and recross it. You cannot keep clear of them. Your helmet pings against them and they try to remove it. Sometimes you have to stop and crawl under wires. Then you wonder what the trench is like in really wet weather. You hear a shell burst at no great distance. You pass two pages of *The Strand Magazine*. Perhaps thirty yards on you pass a cigarette end. After these sensational incidents the trench quiets down again and continues to wind endlessly—just a sandy, extremely narrow vertical walled trench. A giant crack.

At last you reach the front line trench. On an offensive sector it has none of the architectural interest of first line trenches at such places as Soissons or Arras. It was made a week or so ago by joining up shell craters, and if all goes well we move into the German trench along by the line of scraggy trees, at which we peep discreetly, to-morrow night. We can peep discreetly because just at present our guns are putting shrapnel over the enemy at the rate of about three shells a minute, the puffs follow each other up and down the line, and no Germans are staring out to see us.

The Germans "strafed" this trench overnight, and the men are tired and sleepy. Our guns away behind us are doing their best now to give them a rest by strafing the Germans. One or two men are in each forward sap keeping a look out; the rest sleep, a motionless sleep, in the earthy shelter pits that have been scooped out. One officer sits by a telephone under an earth-covered tarpaulin, and a weary man is doing the toilet of a machine gun. We go on to a shallow trench in which we must stoop, and which has been badly knocked about.... Here we have to stop. The road to Berlin is not opened up beyond this point.

My companion on this excursion is a man I have admired for years and never met until I came out to see the war, a fellow writer. He is a journalist let loose. Two-thirds of the junior British officers I met on this journey were really not "army men" at all. One finds that the apparent subaltern is really a musician, or a musical critic, or an Egyptologist, or a solicitor, or a cloth manufacturer, or a writer. At the outbreak of the war my guide dyed his hair to conceal its tell-tale silver, and having been laughed to scorn by the ordinary recruiting people, enlisted in the sportsmen's battalion. He was wounded, and then the authorities discovered that he was likely to be of more use with a commission and drew him, in spite of considerable resistance, out of the firing line. To which he always returns whenever he can get a visitor to take with him as an excuse. He now stood up, fairly high and clear, explaining casually that the Germans were no longer firing, and showed me the points of interest.

I had come right up to No Man's Land at last. It was under my chin. The skyline, the last skyline before the British could look down on Bapaume, showed a mangy wood and a ruined village, crouching under repeated gobbings of British shrapnel. "They've got a battery just there, and we're making it uncomfortable." No Man's Land itself is a weedy space broken up by shell craters, with very little barbed wire in front of us and very little in front of the Germans. "They've got snipers in most of the craters, and you see them at twilight hopping about from one to the other." We have very little wire because we don't mean to stay for very long in this trench, but the Germans have very little wire because they have not been able to get it up yet. They never will get it up now....

I had been led to believe that No Man's Land was littered with the unburied dead, but I saw nothing of the sort at this place. There had been no German counter attack since our men came up here. But at one point as we went along the trench there was a dull stench. "Germans, I think," said my guide, though I did not see how he could tell.

He looked at his watch and remarked reluctantly, "If you start at once, you may just do it."

I wanted to catch the Boulogne boat. It was then just past one in the afternoon. We met the stew as we returned along the communication trench, and it smelt very good indeed.... We hurried across the great spaces of rusty desolation upon which every now and again a German shell was bursting....

That night I was in my flat in London. I had finished reading the accumulated letters of some weeks, and I was just going comfortably to bed.

IV. NEW ARMS FOR OLD ONES

1

Such are the landscapes and method of modern war. It is more difficult in its nature from war as it was waged in the nineteenth century than that was from the nature of the phalanx or the legion. The nucleus fact—when I talked to General Joffre he was very insistent upon this point—is still as ever the ordinary fighting man, but all the accessories and conditions of his personal encounter with the fighting man of the other side have been revolutionised in a quarter of a century. The fighting together in a close disciplined order, shoulder to shoulder, which has held good for thousands of years as the best and most successful fighting, has been destroyed; the idea of *breaking* infantry formation as the chief offensive operation has disappeared, the cavalry charge and the cavalry pursuit are as obsolete as the cross-bow. The modern fighting man is as individualised as a half back or a centre forward in a football team. Personal fighting has become "scrapping" again, an individual adventure with knife, club, bomb, revolver or bayonet. In this war we are working out things instead of thinking them out, and these enormous changes are still but imperfectly apprehended. The trained and specialised military man probably apprehends them as feebly as anyone.

This is a thing that I want to state as emphatically as possible. It is the pith of the lesson I have learnt at the front. The whole method of war has been so altered in the past five and twenty years as to make it a new and different process altogether. Much the larger part of this alteration has only become effective in the last two years. Everyone is a beginner at this new game; everyone is experimenting and learning.

The idea has been put admirably by *Punch*. That excellent picture of the old-fashioned sergeant who complains to his officer of the new recruit; "'E's all right in the trenches, Sir; 'e's all right at a scrap; but 'e won't never make a soldier," is the quintessence of everything I am saying here. And were there not the very gravest doubts about General Smuts in British military circles because he had "had no military training"? A Canadian expressed the new view very neatly on being asked, in consequence of a deficient salute, whether he wanted to be a soldier, by saying, "Not I! I want to be a fighter!"

The professional officer of the old dispensation was a man specialised in relation to one of the established "arms." He was an infantryman, a cavalryman, a gunner or an engineer. It will be interesting to trace the changes that have happened to all these arms.

Before this war began speculative writers had argued that infantry drill in close formation had now no fighting value whatever, that it was no doubt extremely necessary for the handling, packing, forwarding and distribution of men, but that the ideal infantry fighter was now a highly individualised and self-reliant man put into a pit with a machine gun, and supported by a string of other men bringing him up supplies and ready to assist him in any forward rush that might be necessary.

The opening phases of the war seemed to contradict this. It did not at first suit the German game to fight on this most modern theory, and isolated individual action is uncongenial to the ordinary German temperament and opposed to the organised social tendencies of German life. To this day the Germans attack only in close order; they are unable to produce a real modern infantry for aggressive purposes, and it is a matter of astonishment to military minds on the English side that our hastily trained new armies should turn out to be just as good at the new fighting as the most "seasoned troops." But there is no reason whatever why they should not be. "Leading," in the sense of going ahead of the men and making them move about mechanically at the word of command, has ceased. On the British side our magnificent new subalterns and our equally magnificent new non-commissioned officers play the part of captains of football teams; they talk their men individually into an understanding of the job before them; they criticise style and performance. On the French side things have gone even farther. Every man in certain attacks has been given a large scale map of the ground over which he has to go, and has had his own individual job clearly marked and explained to him. All the Allied infantrymen tend to become specialised, as bombers, as machine-gun men, and so on. The unspecialised common soldier, the infantryman who has stood and marched and moved in ranks and ranks, the "serried lines of men," who are the main substance of every battle story for the last three thousand years, are as obsolete as the dodo. The rifle and bayonet very probably are becoming obsolete too. Knives and clubs and revolvers serve better in the trenches. The krees and the Roman sword would be as useful. The fine flourish of the bayonet is only possible in the rare infrequent open. Even the Zulu assegai would serve as well.

The two operations of the infantry attack now are the rush and the "scrap." These come after the artillery preparation. Against the rush, the machine gun is pitted. The machine gun becomes lighter and more and more controllable by one man; as it does so the days of the rifle draw to a close. Against the machine gun we are now directing the "Tank," which goes ahead and puts out the machine gun as soon as it begins to sting the infantry rush. We are also using the swooping aeroplane with a machine gun. Both these devices are of British origin, and they promise very well.

After the rush and the scrap comes the organisation of the captured trench. "Digging in" completes the cycle of modern infantry fighting. You may consider this the first or the last phase of an infantry operation. It is probably at present the least worked-out part of the entire cycle. Here lies the sole German superiority; they bunch and crowd in the rush, they are inferior at the scrap, but they do dig like moles. The weakness of the British is their failure to settle down. They like the rush and the scrap; they press on too far, they get outflanked and lost "in the blue"; they are not naturally clever at the excavating part of the work, and they are not as yet well trained in making dug-outs and shelter-pits rapidly and intelligently. They display most of the faults that were supposed to be most distinctively French before this war came to revolutionise all our conceptions of French character.

2

Now the operations of this modern infantry, which unlike any preceding infantry in the history of war does not fight in disciplined formations but as highly individualised specialists, are determined almost completely by the artillery preparation. Artillery is now the most essential instrument of war. You may still get along with rather bad infantry; you may still hold out even after the loss of the aerial ascendancy, but so soon as your guns fail you approach defeat. The backbone process of the whole art of war is the manufacture in overwhelming quantities, the carriage and delivery of shell upon the vulnerable points of the enemy's positions. That is, so to speak, the essential blow. Even the infantryman is now hardly more than the residuary legatee after the guns have taken their toll.

I have now followed nearly every phase in the life history of a shell from the moment when it is a segment of steel bar just cut off, to the moment when it is no more than a few dispersed and rusting rags and fragments of steel—pressed upon the stray visitor to the battlefield as souvenirs. All good factories are intensely interesting places to visit, but a good munition factory is romantically satisfactory. It is as nearly free from the antagonism of employer and employed as any factory can be. The busy sheds I visited near Paris struck me as being the most living and active things in the entire war machine. Everywhere else I saw fitful activity, or men waiting. I have seen more men sitting about and standing about, more bored inactivity, during my tour than I have ever seen before in my life. Even the front line trenches seem to slumber; the Angel of Death drowses over them, and moves in his sleep to crush out men's lives. The gunfire has an indolent intermittence. But the munition factories grind on night and day, grinding against the factories in Central Europe, grinding out the slow and costly and necessary victory that should end aggressive warfare in the world for ever.

It would be very interesting if one could arrange a meeting between any typical Allied munition maker on the one hand, and the Kaiser and Hindenburg, those two dominant effigies of the German nationalists' dream of "world might." Or failing that, Mr. Dyson might draw the encounter. You imagine these two heroic figures got up for the interview, very magnificent in shining helms and flowing cloaks, decorations, splendid swords, spurs. "Here," one would say, "is the power that has held you. You were bolstered up very loyally by the Krupp firm and so forth, you piled up shell, guns, war material, you hoped to snatch your victory before the industrialisation and invention of the world could turn upon you. But you failed. You were not rapid enough. The battle of the Marne was your misfortune. And Ypres. You lost some chances at Ypres. Two can play at destructive industrialism, and now we out-gun you. We are piling up munitions now faster than you. The essentials of this Game of the War Lord are idiotically simple, but it was not of our choosing. It is now merely a question of months before you make your inevitable admission. This is no war to any great commander's glory. This gentleman in the bowler hat is the victor, Sire; not you. Assisted, Sire, by these disrespectful-looking factory girls in overalls."

For example, there is M. Citroen. Before the war I understand he made automobiles; after the war he wants to turn to and make automobiles again. For the duration of the war he makes shell. He has been temporarily diverted from constructive to destructive industrialism. He did me the honours of his factory. He is a compact, active man in dark clothes and a bowler hat, with a pencil and notebook conveniently at hand. He talked to me in carefully easy French, and watched my face with an intelligent eye through his pince-nez for the signs of comprehension. Then he went on to the next point.

He took me through every stage of his process. In his office he showed me the general story. Here were photographs of certain vacant fields and old sheds—"this place"—he indicated the altered prospect from the window—"at the outbreak of the war." He showed me a plan of the first undertaking. "Now we have rather over nine thousand workpeople."

He showed me a little row of specimens. "These we make for Italy. These go to Russia. These are the Rumanian pattern."

Thence to the first stage, the chopping up of the iron bars, the furnace, the punching out of the first shape of the shell; all this is men's work. I had seen this sort of thing before in peace ironworks, but I saw it again with the same astonishment, the absolute precision of movement on the part of the half-naked sweating men, the calculated efficiency of each worker, the apparent heedlessness, the real certitude, with which the blazing hot cylinder is put here, dropped there, rolls to its next appointed spot, is chopped up and handed on, the swift passage to the cooling crude, pinkish-purple shell shape. Down a long line one sees in perspective a practical symmetry, of furnace and machine group and the shells marching on from this first series of phases to undergo the long succession of operations, machine after machine, across the great width of the shed in which eighty per cent of the workers are women. There is a thick dust of sounds in the air, a rumble of shafting, sudden thuddings, clankings, and M. Citroen has to raise his voice. He points out where he has made little changes in procedures, cut out some wasteful movement.... He has an idea and makes a note in the ever-ready notebook.

There is a beauty about all these women, there is extraordinary grace in their finely adjusted movements. I have come from an after-lunch coffee upon the boulevards and from watching the ugly fashion of our time; it is a relief to be reminded that most women can after all be beautiful—if only they would not "dress." these women wear simple overalls and caps. In the cap is a rosette. Each shed has its own colour of rosette.

"There is much esprit de corps here," says M. Citroen.

"And also," he adds, showing obverse as well as reverse of the world's problem of employment and discipline, "we can see at once if a woman is not in her proper shed."

Across the great sheds under the shafting—how fine it must look at night!—the shells march, are shaped, cut, fitted with copper bands, calibrated, polished, varnished....

Then we go on to another system of machines in which lead is reduced to plastic ribbons and cut into shrapnel bullets as the sweetstuff makers pull out and cut up sweetstuff. And thence into a warren of hot underground passages in which run the power cables. There is not a cable in the place that is not immediately accessible to the electricians. We visit the dynamos and a vast organisation of switchboards....

These things are more familiar to M. Citroen than they are to me. He wants me to understand, but he does not realise that I would like a little leisure to wonder. What is interesting him just now, because it is the newest thing, is his method of paying his workers. He lifts a hand gravely: "I said, what we must do is abolish altogether the counting of change."

At a certain hour, he explained, came pay-time. The people had done; it was to his interest and their that they should get out of the works as quickly as possible and rest and amuse themselves. He watched them standing in queues at the wickets while inside someone counted; so many francs, so many centimes. It bored him to see this useless, tiresome waiting. It is abolished. Now at the end of each week the worker goes to a window under the initial of his name, and is handed a card on which these items have been entered:

Balance from last week. So many hours at so much. Premiums.

The total is so many francs, so many centimes. This is divided into the nearest round number, 100, 120, 80 francs as the case may be, and a balance of the odd francs and centimes. The latter is carried forward to the next week's account. At the bottom of the card is a tear-off coupon with a stamp, coloured to indicate the round sum, green, let us say, for 100, blue for 130 francs. This is taken to a wicket marked 100 or 130 as the case may be, and there stands a cashier with his money in piles of 100 or 130 francs counted ready to hand; he sweeps in the coupon, sweeps out the cash. "*Next!*"

I became interested in the worker's side of this organisation. I insist on seeing the entrances, the clothes-changing places, the lavatories, and so forth of the organisation. As we go about we pass a string of electric trolleys steered by important-looking girls, and loaded with shell, finished as far as these works are concerned and on their way to the railway siding. We visit the hospital, for these works demand a medical staff. It is not only that men and women faint or fall ill, but there are accidents, burns, crushings, and the like. The war casualties begin already here, and they fall chiefly among the women. I saw a wounded woman with a bandaged face sitting very quietly in the corner.

The women here face danger, perhaps not quite such obvious danger as the women who, at the next stage in the shell's career, make and pack the explosives in their silk casing, but quite considerable risk. And they work with a real enthusiasm. They know they are fighting the Bloches as well as any men. Certain of them wear Russian decorations. The women of this particular factory have been thanked by the Tsar, and a number of decorations were sent by him for distribution among them.

3

The shell factory and the explosives shed stand level with the drill yard as the real first stage in one of the two essential *punches* in modern war. When one meets the shell again it is being unloaded from the railway truck into an ammunition dump. And here the work of control is much more the work of a good traffic manager than of the old-fashioned soldier.

The dump I best remember I visited on a wet and windy day. Over a great space of ground the sidings of the rail-head spread, the normal gauge rail-head spread out like a fan and interdigitated with the narrow gauge lines that go up practically to the guns. And also at the sides camions were loading, and an officer from the Midi in charge of one of these was being dramatically indignant at five minutes' delay. Between these two sets of lines, shells were piled of all sizes, I should think some hundreds of thousands of shells altogether, wet and shining in the rain. French reservists, soldiers from Madagascar, and some Senegalese were busy at different points loading and unloading the precious freights. A little way from me were despondent-looking German prisoners handling timber. All this dump was no more than an eddy as it were in the path of the shell from its birth from the steel bars near Paris to the accomplishment of its destiny in the destruction or capture of more Germans.

And next the visitor meets the shell coming up upon a little trolley to the gun. He sees the gunners, as drilled and precise as the men he saw at the forges, swing out the breech block and run the shell, which has met and combined with its detonators and various other industrial products since it left the main dump, into the gun. The breech closes like a safe door, and hides the shell from the visitor. It is "good-bye." He receives exaggerated warning of the danger to his ears, stuffs his fingers into them, and opens his mouth as instructed, hears a loud but by no means deafening report, and sees a spit of flame near the breech. Regulations of a severe character prevent his watching from an aeroplane the delivery of the goods upon the customers opposite.

I have already described the method of locating enemy guns and so forth by photography. Many of the men at this work are like dentists rather than soldiers; they are busy in carefully lit rooms, they wear white overalls, they have clean hands and laboratory manners. The only really romantic figure in the whole of this process, the only figure that has anything of the old soldierly swagger about him still, is the aviator. And, as one friend remarked to me when I visited the work of the British flying corps, "The real essential strength of this arm is the organisation of its repairs. Here is one of the repair vans through which our machine guns go. It is a motor workshop on wheels. But at any time all this park, everything, can pack up and move forward like Barnum and Bailey's Circus. The machine guns come through this shop in rotation; they go out again, cleaned, repaired, made new again. Since we got all that working we have heard nothing of a machine gun jamming in any air fight at all."...

The rest of the career of the shell after it has left the gun one must imagine chiefly from the incoming shell from the enemy. You see suddenly a flying up of earth and stones and anything else that is movable in the neighbourhood of the shell-burst, the instantaneous unfolding of a dark cloud of dust and reddish smoke, which comes very quickly to a certain size and then begins slowly to fray out and blow away. Then, after seeing the cloud of the burst you hear the hiss of the shell's approach, and finally you are hit by the sound of the explosion. This is the climax and end of the life history of any shell that is not a dud shell. Afterwards the battered fuse may serve as some journalist's paper-weight. The rest is scrap iron.

Such is, so to speak, the primary process of modern warfare. I will not draw the obvious pacifist moral of the intense folly of human concentration upon such a process. The Germans willed it. We Allies have but obeyed the German will for warfare because we could not do otherwise, we have taken up this simple game of shell delivery, and we are teaching them that we can play it better, in the hope that so we and the world may be freed from the German will-to-power and all its humiliating and disgusting consequences henceforth for ever. Europe now is no more than a household engaged in holding up and if possible overpowering a monomaniac member.

4

Now the whole of this process of the making and delivery of a shell, which is the main process of modern warfare, is one that can be far better conducted by a man accustomed to industrial organisation or transit work than by the old type of soldier. This is a thing that cannot be too plainly stated or too often repeated. Germany nearly won this way because of her tremendously modern industrial resources; but she blundered into it and she is losing it because she has too many men in military uniform and because their tradition and interests were to powerful with her. All the state and glories of soldiering, the bright uniforms, the feathers and spurs, the flags, the march-past, the disciplined massed advance, the charge; all these are as needless and obsolete now in war as the masks and shields of an old-time Chinese brave. Liberal-minded people talk of the coming dangers of militarism in the face of events that prove conclusively that professional militarism is already as dead as Julius Caesar. What is coming is not so much the conversion of men into soldiers as the socialisation of the economic organisation of the country with a view to both national and international necessities. We do not want to turn a chemist or a photographer into a little figure like a lead soldier, moving mechanically at the word of command, but we do want to make his chemistry or photography swiftly available if the national organisation is called upon to fight.

We have discovered that the modern economic organisation is in itself a fighting machine. It is so much so that it is capable of taking on and defeating quite easily any merely warrior people that is so rash as to pit itself against it. Within the last sixteen years methods of fighting have been elaborated that have made war an absolutely hopeless adventure for any barbaric or non-industrialised people. In the rush of larger events few people have realised the significance of the rapid squashing of the Senussi in western Egypt, and the collapse of De Wet's rebellion in South Africa. Both these struggles would have been long, tedious and uncertain even in A.D. 1900. This time they have been, so to speak, child's play.

Occasionally into the writer's study there come to hand drifting fragments of the American literature upon the question of "preparedness," and American papers discussing the Mexican situation. In none of these is there evident any clear realisation of the fundamental revolution that has occurred in military methods during the last two years. It looks as if a Mexican war, for example, was thought of as an affair of rather imperfectly trained young men with rifles and horses and old-fashioned things like that. A Mexican war on that level might be as tedious as the South African war. But if the United States preferred to go into Mexican affairs with what I may perhaps call a 1916 autumn outfit instead of the small 1900 outfit she seems to possess at present, there is no reason why America should not clear up any and every Mexican guerilla force she wanted to in a few weeks.

To do that she would need a plant of a few hundred aeroplanes, for the most part armed with machine guns, and the motor repair vans and so forth needed to go with the aeroplanes; she would need a comparatively small army of infantry armed with machine guns, with motor transport, and a few small land ironclads. Such a force could locate, overtake, destroy and disperse any possible force that a country in the present industrial condition of Mexico could put into the field. No sort of entrenchment or fortification possible in Mexico could stand against it. It could go from one end of the country to the other without serious loss, and hunt down and capture anyone it wished....

The practical political consequence of the present development of warfare, of the complete revolution in the conditions of warfare since this century began, is to make war absolutely hopeless for any peoples not able either to manufacture or procure the very complicated appliances and munitions now needed for its prosecution. Countries like Mexico, Bulgaria, Serbia, Afghanistan or Abyssinia are no more capable of going to war without the connivance and help of manufacturing states than horses are capable of flying. And this makes possible such a complete control of war by the few great states which are at the necessary level of industrial development as not the most Utopian of us have hitherto dared to imagine.

5

Infantrymen with automobile transport, plentiful machine guns, Tanks and such-like accessories; that is the first Arm in modern war. The factory hand and all the material of the shell route from the factory to the gun constitute the second Arm. Thirdly comes the artillery, the guns and the photographic aeroplanes working with the guns. Next I suppose we must count sappers and miners as a fourth Arm of greatly increased importance. The fifth and last combatant Arm is the modern substitute for cavalry; and that also is essentially a force of aeroplanes supported by automobiles. Several of the French leaders with whom I talked seemed to be convinced that the horse is absolutely done with in modern warfare. There is nothing, they declared, that cavalry ever did that cannot now be done better by aeroplane.

This is something to break the hearts of the Prussian junkers and of old-fashioned British army people. The hunt across the English countryside, the preservation of the fox as a sacred animal, the race meeting, the stimulation of betting in all classes of the public; all these things depend ultimately upon the proposition that the "breed of horses" is of vital importance to the military strength of Great Britain. But if the arguments of these able French soldiers are sound, the cult of the horse ceases to be of any more value to England than the elegant activities of the Toxophilite Society. Moreover, there has been a colossal buying of horses for the British army, a tremendous organisation for the purchase and supply of fodder, then employment of tens of thousands of men as grooms, minders and the like, who would otherwise have been in the munition factories or the trenches.

To what possible use can cavalry be put? Can it be used in attack? Not against trenches; that is better done by infantrymen following up gunfire. Can it be used against broken infantry in the open? Not if the enemy has one or two machine guns covering their retreat. Against expose infantry the swooping aeroplane with a machine gun is far more deadly and more difficult to hit. Behind it your infantry can follow to receive surrenders; in most circumstances they can come up on cycles if it is a case of getting up quickly across a wide space. Similarly for pursuit the use of wire and use of the machine gun have abolished the possibility of a pouring cavalry charge. The swooping aeroplane does everything that cavalry can do in the way of disorganising the enemy, and far more than it can do in the way of silencing machine guns. It can capture guns in retreat much more easily by bombing traction engines and coming down low and shooting horses and men. An ideal modern pursuit would be an advance of guns, automobiles full of infantry, motor cyclists and cyclists, behind a high screen of observation aeroplanes and a low screen of bombing and fighting aeroplanes. Cavalry *might* advance across fields and so forth, but only as a very accessory part of the general advance....

And what else is there for the cavalry to do?

It may be argued that horses can go over country that is impossible for automobiles. That is to ignore altogether what has been done in this war by such devices as caterpillar wheels. So far from cavalry being able to negotiate country where machines would stick and fail, mechanism can now ride over places where any horse would flounder.

I submit these considerations to the horse-lover. They are not my original observations; they have been put to me and they have convinced me. Except perhaps as a parent of transport mules I see no further part henceforth for the horse to play in war.

6

The form and texture of the coming warfare—if there is still warfare to come—are not yet to be seen in their completeness upon the modern battlefield. One swallow does not make a summer, nor a handful of aeroplanes, a "Tank" or so, a few acres of shell craters, and a village here and there, pounded out of recognition, do more than foreshadow the spectacle of modernised war on land. War by these developments has become the monopoly of the five great industrial powers; it is their alternative to end or evolve it, and if they continue to disagree, then it must needs become a spectacle of majestic horror such as no man can yet conceive. It has been wise of Mr. Pennell therefore, who has recently been drawing his impressions of the war upon stone, to make his pictures not upon the battlefield, but among the huge industrial apparatus that is thrusting behind and thrusting up through the war of the gentlemen in spurs. He gives us the splendours and immensities of forge and gun pit, furnace and mine shaft. He shows you how great they are and how terrible. Among them go the little figures of men, robbed of all dominance, robbed of all individual quality. He leaves it for you to draw the obvious conclusion that presently, if we cannot contrive to put an end to war, blacknessess like these, enormities and flares and towering threats, will follow in the track of the Tanks and come trampling over the bickering confusion of mankind.

There is something very striking in these insignificant and incidental men that Mr. Pennell shows us. Nowhere does a man dominate in all these wonderful pictures. You may argue perhaps that that is untrue to the essential realities; all this array of machine and workshop, all this marshalled power and purpose, has been the creation of inventor and business organiser. But are we not a little too free with that word *"creation"*? Falstaff was a "creation" perhaps, or the Sistine sibyls; there we have indubitably an end conceived and sought and achieved; but did these inventors and business organisers do more than heed certain unavoidable imperatives? Seeking coal they were obliged to mine in a certain way; seeking steel they had to do this and this and not that and that; seeking profit they had to obey the imperative of the economy. So little did they plan their ends that most of these manufacturers speak with a kind of astonishment of the deadly use to which their works are put. They find themselves making the new war as a man might wake out of some drugged condition to find himself strangling his mother.

So that Mr. Pennell's sketchy and transient human figures seem altogether right to me. He sees these forges, workshops, cranes and the like, as inhuman and as wonderful as cliffs or great caves or icebergs or the stars. They are a new aspect of the logic of physical necessity that made all these older things, and he seizes upon the majesty and beauty of their dimensions with an entire impartiality. And they are as impartial. Through all these lithographs runs one present motif, the motif of the supreme effort of western civilisation to save itself and the world from the dominance of the reactionary German Imperialism of modern science. The pictures are arranged to shape out the life of a shell, from the mine to the great gun; nothing remains of their history to show except the ammunition dump, the gun in action and the shell-burst. Upon this theme all these great appearances are strung to-day. But to-morrow they may be strung upon some other and nobler purpose. These gigantic beings of which the engineer is the master and slave, are neither benevolent nor malignant. To-day they produce destruction, they are the slaves of the spur; to-morrow we hope they will bridge and carry and house and help again.

For that peace we struggle against the dull inflexibility of the German Will-to-Power.

V. TANKS

1

It is the British who have produced the "land ironclad" since I returned from France, and used it apparently with very good effect. I felt no little chagrin at not seeing them there, because I have a peculiar interest in these contrivances. It would be more than human not to claim a little in this matter. I described one in a story in *The Strand Magazine* in 1903, and my story could stand in parallel columns beside the first account of these monsters in action given by Mr. Beach Thomas or Mr. Philip Gibbs. My friend M. Joseph Reinach has successfully passed off long extracts from my story as descriptions of the Tanks upon British officers who had just seen them. The filiation was indeed quite traceable. They were my grandchildren—I felt a little like King Lear when first I read about them. Yet let me state at once that I was certainly not their prime originator. I took up an idea, manipulated it slightly, and handed it on. The idea was suggested to me by the contrivances of a certain Mr. Diplock, whose "ped-rail" notion, the notion of a wheel that was something more than a wheel, a wheel that would take locomotives up hill-sides and over ploughed fields, was public property nearly twenty years ago. Possibly there were others before Diplock. To the Ped-rail also Commander Murray Sueter, one of the many experimentalists upon the early tanks, admits his indebtedness, and it would seem that Mr. Diplock was actually concerned in the earlier stage of the tanks.

Since my return I have been able to see the Tank at home, through the courtesy of the Ministry of Munitions. They have progressed far beyond any recognisable resemblance to the initiatives of Mr. Diplock; they have approximated rather to the American caterpillar. As I suspected when first I heard of these devices, the War Office and the old army people had practically nothing to do with their development. They took to it very reluctantly—as they have taken to every novelty in this war. One brilliant general scrawled over an early proposal the entirely characteristic comment that it was a pity the inventor could not use his imagination to better purpose. (That foolish British trick of sneering at "imagination" has cost us hundreds of thousands of useless casualties and may yet lose us the war.) Tanks were first mooted at the front about a year and a half ago; Mr. Winston Churchill was then asking questions about their practicability; he filled many simple souls with terror; they thought him a most dangerous lunatic. The actual making of the Tanks arose as an irregular side development of the armoured-car branch of the Royal Naval Air Service work. The names most closely associated with the work are (I quote a reply of Dr. Macnamara's in the House of Commons) Mr. d'Eyncourt, the Director of Naval Construction, Mr. W. O. Tritton, Lieut. Wilson, R.N.A.S., Mr. Bussell, Lieut. Stern, R.N.A.S., who is now Colonel Stern, Captain Symes, and Mr. F. Skeens. There are many other claims too numerous to mention in detail.

But however much the Tanks may disconcert the gallant Colonel Newcomes who throw an air of restraint over our victorious front, there can be no doubt that they are an important as well as a novel development of the modern offensive. Of course neither the Tanks nor their very obvious next developments going to wrest the decisive pre-eminence from the aeroplane. The aeroplane remains now more than ever the instrument of victory upon the western front. Aerial ascendancy, properly utilised, is victory. But the mobile armoured big gun and the Tank as a machine-gun silencer must enormously facilitate an advance against the blinded enemy. Neither of them can advance against properly aimed big gun fire. That has to be disposed of before they make their entrance. It remains the function of the aeroplane to locate the hostile big guns and to direct the *tir de demolition* upon them before the advance begins—possibly even to bomb them out. But hitherto, after the destruction of driving back of the defender's big guns has been effected, the dug-out and the machine gun have still inflicted heavy losses upon the advancing infantry until the fight is won. So soon as the big guns are out, the tanks will advance, destroying machine guns, completing the destruction of the wire, and holding prisoners immobile. Then the infantry will follow to gather in the sheaves. Multitudinously produced and—I write it with a defiant eye on Colonel Newcome—*properly handled*, these land ironclads are going to do very great things in shortening the war, in pursuit, in breaking up the retreating enemy. Given the air ascendancy, and I am utterly unable to imagine any way of conclusively stopping or even greatly delaying an offensive thus equipped.

2

The young of even the most horrible beasts have something piquant and engaging about them, and so I suppose it is in the way of things that the land ironclad which opens a new and more dreadful and destructive phase in the human folly of warfare, should appear first as if it were a joke. Never has any such thing so completely masked its wickedness under an appearance of genial silliness. The Tank is a creature to which one naturally flings a pet name; the five or six I was shown wandering, rooting and climbing over obstacles, round a large field near X, were as amusing and disarming as a little of lively young pigs.

At first the War Office prevented the publication of any pictures or descriptions of these contrivances except abroad; then abruptly the embargo was relaxed, and the press was flooded with photographs. The reader will be familiar now with their appearance. They resemble large slugs with an underside a little like the flattened rockers of a rocking-horse, slugs between 20 and 40 feet long. They are like flat-sided slugs, slugs of spirit, who raise an enquiring snout, like the snout of a dogfish, into the air. They crawl upon their bellies in a way that would be tedious to describe to the general reader and unnecessary to describe to the enquiring specialists. They go over the ground with the sliding speed of active snails. Behind them trail two wheels, supporting a flimsy tail, wheels that strike one as incongruous as if a monster began kangaroo and ended doll's perambulator. (These wheels annoy me.) They are not steely monsters; they are painted with drab and unassuming colours that are fashionable in modern warfare, so that the armour seems rather like the integument of a rhinoceros. At the sides of the head project armoured checks, and from above these stick out guns that look like stalked eyes. That is the general appearance of the contemporary tank.

It slides on the ground; the silly little wheels that so detract from the genial bestiality of its appearance dandle and bump behind it. It swings about its axis. It comes to an obstacle, a low wall let us say, or a heap of bricks, and sets to work to climb it with its snout. It rears over the obstacle, it raises its straining belly, it overhangs more and more, and at last topples forward; it sways upon the heap and then goes plunging downwards, sticking out the weak counterpoise of its wheeled tail. If it comes to a house or a tree or a wall or such-like obstruction it rams against it so as to bring all its weight to bear upon it—it weighs *some* tons—and then climbs over the debris. I saw it, and incredulous soldiers of experience watched it at the same time, cross trenches and wallow amazingly through muddy exaggerations of small holes. Then I repeated the tour inside.

Again the Tank is like a slug. The slug, as every biological student knows, is unexpectedly complicated inside. The Tank is as crowded with inward parts as a battleship. It is filled with engines, guns and ammunition, and in the interstices men.

"You will smash your hat," said Colonel Stern. "No; keep it on, or else you will smash your head."

Only Mr. C. R. W. Nevinson could do justice to the interior of a Tank. You see a hand gripping something; you see the eyes and forehead of an engineer's face; you perceive that an overall bluishness beyond the engine is the back of another man. "Don't hold that," says someone; "it is too hot. Hold on to that." The engines roar, so loudly that I doubt whether one could hear guns without; the floor begins to slope and slopes until one seems to be at forty-five degrees or thereabouts; then the whole concern swings up and sways and slants the other way. You have crossed a bank. You heel sideways. Through the door which has been left open you see the little group of engineers, staff officers and naval men receding and falling away behind you. You straighten up and go up hill. You halt and begin to rotate. Through the open door, the green field, with its red walls, rows of worksheds and forests of chimneys in the background, begins a steady processional movement. The group of engineers and officers and naval men appears at the other side of the door and farther off. Then comes a sprint down hill. You descend and stretch your legs.

About the field other Tanks are doing their stunts. One is struggling in an apoplectic way in the mud pit with a cheek half buried. It noses its way out and on with an air of animal relief.

They are like jokes by Heath Robinson. One forgets that these things have already saved the lives of many hundreds of our soldiers and smashed and defeated thousands of Germans.

Said one soldier to me: "In the old attacks you used to see the British dead lying outside the machine-gun emplacements like birds outside a butt with a good shot inside. *Now,* these things walk through."

3

I saw other things that day at X. The Tank is only a beginning in a new phase of warfare. Of these other things I may only write in the most general terms.

But though Tanks and their collaterals are being made upon a very considerable scale in X, already I realised as I walked through gigantic forges as high and marvellous as cathedrals, and from workshed to workshed where gun carriages, ammunition carts and a hundred such things were flowing into existence with the swelling abundance of a river that flows out of a gorge, that as the demand for the new developments grows clear and strong, the resources of Britain are capable still of a tremendous response. *If only we do not rob these great factories and works of their men.*

Upon this question certain things need to be said very plainly. The decisive factor in the sort of war we are now waging is production and right use of mechanical material; victory in this war depends now upon three things: the aeroplane, the gun, and the Tank developments. These—and not crowds of men—are the prime necessity for a successful offensive. Every man we draw from munition making to the ranks brings our western condition nearer to the military condition of Russia. In these things we may be easily misled by military "experts" We have to remember that the military "expert" is a man who learnt his business before 1914, and that the business of war has been absolutely revolutionised since 1914; the military expert is a man trained to think of war as essentially an affair of cavalry, infantry in formation, and field guns, whereas cavalry is entirely obsolete, infantry no longer fights in formation, and the methods of gunnery have been entirely changed. The military man I observe still runs about the world in spurs, he travels in trains in spurs, he walks in spurs, he thinks in terms of spurs. He has still to discover that it is about as ridiculous as if he were to carry a crossbow. I take it these spurs are only the outward and visible sign of an inward obsolescence. The disposition of the military "expert" is still to think too little of machinery and to demand too much of the men. Behind our front at the time of my visit there were, for example, many thousands of cavalry, men tending horses, men engaged in transporting bulky fodder for horses and the like. These men were doing about as much in this war as if they had been at Timbuctoo. Every man who is taken from munition making at X to spur-worshipping in khaki, is a dead loss to the military efficiency of the country. Every man that is needed or is likely to be needed for the actual operations of modern warfare can be got by combing out the cavalry, the brewing and distilling industries, the theatres and music halls, and the like unproductive occupations. The under-staffing of munition works, the diminution of their efficiency by the use of aged and female labour, is the straight course to failure in this war.

In X, in the forges and machine shops, I saw already too large a proportion of boys and grey heads.

War is a thing that changes very rapidly, and we have in the Tanks only the first of a great series of offensive developments. They are bound to be improved, at a great pace. The method of using them will change very rapidly. Any added invention will necessitate the scrapping of old types and the production of the new patterns in quantity. It is of supreme necessity to the Allies if they are to win this war outright that the lead in inventions and enterprise which the British have won over the Germans in this matter should be retained. It is our game now to press the advantage for all it is worth. We have to keep ahead to win. We cannot do so unless we have unstinted men and unstinted material to produce each new development as its use is realised.

Given that much, the Tank will enormously enhance the advantage of the new offensive method on the French front; the method that is of gun demolition after aerial photography, followed by an advance; it is a huge addition to our prospect of decisive victory. What does it do? It solves two problems. The existing Tank affords a means of advancing against machine-gun fire and of destroying wire and machine guns without much risk of loss, so soon as the big guns have done their duty by the enemy guns. And also behind the Tank itself, it is useless to conceal, lies the possibility of bringing up big guns and big gun ammunition, across nearly any sort of country, as fast as the advance can press forward. Hitherto every advance has paid a heavy toll to the machine gun, and every advance has had to halt after a couple of miles or so while the big guns (taking five or six days for the job) toiled up to the new positions.

4

It is impossible to restrain a note of sharp urgency from what one has to say about these developments. The Tanks remove the last technical difficulties in our way to decisive victory and a permanent peace; they also afford a reason for straining every nerve to bring about a decision and peace soon. At the risk of seeming an imaginative alarmist I would like to point out the reasons these things disclose for hurrying this war to a decision and doing our utmost to arrange the world's affairs so as to make another war improbable. Already these serio-comic Tanks, weighing something over twenty tons or so, have gone slithering around and sliding over dead and wounded men. That is not an incident for sensitive minds to dwell upon, but it is a mere little child's play anticipation of what the big land ironclads *that are bound to come if there is no world pacification*, are going to do.

What lies behind the Tank depends upon this fact; there is no definable upward limit of mass. Upon that I would lay all the stress possible, because everything turns upon that.

You cannot make a land ironclad so big and heavy but that you cannot make a caterpillar track wide enough and strong enough to carry it forward. Tanks are quite possible that will carry twenty-inch or twenty-five inch guns, besides minor armament. Such Tanks may be undesirable; the production may exceed the industrial resources of any empire to produce; but there is no inherent impossibility in such things. There are not even the same limitations as to draught and docking accommodation that sets bounds to the size of battleships. It follows, therefore, as a necessary deduction that if the world's affairs are so left at the end of the war that the race of armaments continues, that Tank will develop steadily into a tremendous instrument of warfare, driven by engines of scores of thousands of horse-power, tracking on a track scores of hundreds of yards wide and weighing hundreds or thousands of tons. Nothing but a world agreement not to do so can prevent this logical development of the land ironclad. Such a structure will make wheel-ruts scores of feet deep; it will plough up, devastate and destroy the country it passes over altogether.

For my own part I never imagined the land ironclad idea would get loose into war. I thought that the military intelligence was essentially unimaginative and that such an aggressive military power as Germany, dominated by military people, would never produce anything of the sort. I thought that this war would be fought out without Tanks and that then war would come to an end. For of course it is mere stupidity that makes people doubt the ultimate ending of war. I have been so far justified in these expectations of mine, that it is not from military sources that these things have come. They have been thrust upon the soldiers from without. But now that they are loose, now that they are in war, we have to face their full possibilities, to use our advantage in them and press on to the end of the war. In support of a photo-aero directed artillery, even our present Tanks can be used to complete an invisible offensive. We shall not so much push as ram. It is doubtful if the Germans can get anything of the sort into action before six months are out. We ought to get the war on to German soil before the Tanks have grown to more than three or four times their present size. Then it will not matter so much how much bigger they grow. It will be the German landscape that will suffer.

After one has seen the actual Tanks it is not very difficult to close one's eyes and figure the sort of Tank that may be arguing with Germany in a few months' time about the restoration of Belgium and Serbia and France, the restoration of the sunken tonnage, the penalties of the various Zeppelin and submarine murders, the freedom of seas and land alike from piracy, the evacuation of all Poland including Posen and Cracow, and the guarantees for the future peace of Europe. The machine will be perhaps as big as a destroyer and more heavily armed and equipped. It will swim over and through the soil at a pace of ten or twelve miles an hour. In front of it will be corn, land, neat woods, orchards, pasture, gardens, villages and towns. It will advance upon its belly with a swaying motion, devouring the ground beneath it. Behind it masses of soil and rock, lumps of turf, splintered wood, bits of houses, occasional streaks of red, will drop from its track, and it will leave a wake, six or seven times as wide as a high road, from which all soil, all cultivation, all semblance to cultivated or cultivatable land will have disappeared. It will not even be a track of soil. It will be a track of subsoil laid bare. It will be a flayed strip of nature. In the course of its fighting the monster may have to turnabout. It will then halt and spin slowly round, grinding out an arena of desolation with a diameter equal to its length. If it has to retreat and advance again these streaks and holes of destruction will increase and multiply. Behind the fighting line these monsters will manoeuvre to and fro, destroying the land for all ordinary agricultural purposes for ages to come. The first imaginative account of the land ironclad that was ever written concluded with the words, "They are the *reductio ad absurdum* of war." They are, and it is to the engineers, the ironmasters, the workers and the inventive talent of Great Britain and

France that we must look to ensure that it is in Germany, the great teacher of war, that this demonstration of war's ultimate absurdity is completed.

For forty years Frankenstein Germany invoked war, turned every development of material and social science to aggressive ends, and at last when she felt the time was ripe she let loose the new monster that she had made of war to cow the spirit of mankind. She set the thing trampling through Belgium. She cannot grumble if at last it comes home, stranger and more dreadful even than she made it, trampling the German towns and fields with German blood upon it and its eyes towards Berlin.

This logical development of the Tank idea may seem a gloomy prospect for mankind. But it is open to question whether the tremendous development of warfare that has gone on in the last two years does after all open a prospect of unmitigated gloom. There has been a good deal of cheap and despondent sneering recently at the phrase, "The war that will end war." It is still possible to maintain that that may be a correct description of this war. It has to be remembered that war, as the aeroplane and the Tank have made it, has already become an impossible luxury for any barbaric or uncivilised people. War on the grade that has been achieved on the Somme predicates an immense industrialism behind it. Of all the States in the world only four can certainly be said to be fully capable of sustaining war at the level to which it has now been brought upon the western front. These are Britain, France, Germany, and the United States of America. Less certainly equal to the effort are Italy, Japan, Russia, and Austria. These eight powers are the only powers *capable of warfare under modern conditions*. Five are already Allies and one is incurably pacific. There is no other power or people in the world that can go to war now without the consent and connivance of these great powers. If we consider their alliances, we may count it that the matter rests now between two groups of Allies and one neutral power. So that while on the one hand the development of modern warfare of which the Tank is the present symbol opens a prospect of limitless senseless destruction, it opens on the other hand a prospect of organised world control. This Tank development must ultimately bring the need of a real permanent settlement within the compass of the meanest of diplomatic intelligences. A peace that will restore competitive armaments has now become a less desirable prospect for everyone than a continuation of the war. Things were bad enough before, when the land forces were still in a primitive phase of infantry, cavalry and artillery, and when the only real race to develop monsters and destructors was for sea power. But the race for sea power before 1914 was mere child's play to the breeding of engineering monstrosities for land warfare that must now follow any indeterminate peace settlement. I am no blind believer in the wisdom of mankind, but I cannot believe that men are so insensate and headstrong as to miss the plain omens of the present situation.

So that after all the cheerful amusement the sight of a Tank causes may not be so very unreasonable. These things may be no more than one of those penetrating flashes of wit that will sometimes light up and dispel the contentions of an angry man. If they are not that, then they are the grimmest jest that ever set men grinning. Wait and see, if you do not believe me.

HOW PEOPLE THINK ABOUT THE WAR

I. DO THEY REALLY THINK AT ALL?

All human affairs are mental affairs; the bright ideas of to-day are the realities of to-morrow. The real history of mankind is the history of how ideas have arisen, how they have taken possession of men's minds, how they have struggled, altered, proliferated, decayed. There is nothing in this war at all but a conflict of ideas, traditions, and mental habits. The German Will clothed in conceptions of aggression and fortified by cynical falsehood, struggles against the fundamental sanity of the German mind and the confused protest of mankind. So that the most permanently important thing in the tragic process of this war is the change of opinion that is going on. What are people making of it? Is it producing any great common understandings, any fruitful unanimities?

No doubt it is producing enormous quantities of cerebration, but is it anything more than chaotic and futile cerebration? We are told all sorts of things in answer to that, things without a scrap of evidence or probability to support them. It is, we are assured, turning people to religion, making them moral and thoughtful. It is also, we are assured with equal confidence, turning them to despair and moral disaster. It will be followed by (1) a period of moral renascence, and (2) a debauch. It is going to make the workers (1) more and (2) less obedient and industrious. It is (1) inuring men to war and (2) filling them with a passionate resolve never to suffer war again. And so on. I propose now to ask what is really happening in this matter? How is human opinion changing? I have opinions of my own and they are bound to colour my discussion. The reader must allow for that, and as far as possible I will remind him where necessary to make his allowance.

Now first I would ask, is any really continuous and thorough mental process going on at all about this war? I mean, is there any considerable number of people who are seeing it as a whole, taking it in as a whole, trying to get a general idea of it from which they can form directing conclusions for the future? Is there any considerable number of people even trying to do that? At any rate let me point out first that there is quite an enormous mass of people who—in spite of the fact that their minds are concentrated on aspects of this war, who are at present hearing, talking, experiencing little else than the war—are nevertheless neither doing nor trying to do anything that deserves to be called thinking about it at all. They may even be suffering quite terribly by it. But they are no more mastering its causes, reasons, conditions, and the possibility of its future prevention than a monkey that has been rescued in a scorching condition from the burning of a house will have mastered the problem of a fire. It is just happening to and about them. It may, for anything they have learnt about it, happen to them again.

A vast majority of people are being swamped by the spectacular side of the business. It was very largely my fear of being so swamped myself that made me reluctant to go as a spectator to the front. I knew that my chances of being hit by a bullet were infinitesimal, but I was extremely afraid of being hit by some too vivid impression. I was afraid that I might see some horribly wounded man or some decayed dead body that would so scar my memory and stamp such horror into me as to reduce me to a mere useless, gibbering, stop-the-war-at-any-price pacifist. Years ago my mind was once darkened very badly for some weeks with a kind of fear and distrust of life through a sudden unexpected encounter one tranquil evening with a drowned body. But in this journey in Italy and France, although I have had glimpses of much death and seen many wounded men, I have had no really horrible impressions at all. That side of the business has, I think, been overwritten. The thing that haunts me most is the impression of a prevalent relapse into extreme untidiness, of a universal discomfort, of fields, and of ruined houses treated disregardfully.... But that is not what concerns us now in this discussion. What concerns us now is the fact that this war is producing spectacular effects so tremendous and incidents so strange, so remarkable, so vivid, that the mind forgets both causes and consequences and simply sits down to stare.

For example, there is this business of the Zeppelin raids in England. It is a supremely silly business; it is the most conclusive demonstration of the intellectual inferiority of the German to the Western European that is should ever have happened. There was the clearest *a priori* case against the gas-bag. I remember the discussions ten or twelve years ago in which it was established to the satisfaction of every reasonable man that ultimately the "heavier than air" machine (as we called it then) must fly better than the gas-bag, and still more conclusively that no gas-bag was conceivable that could hope to fight and defeat aeroplanes. Nevertheless the German, with that dull faith of his in mere "Will," persisted along his line. He knew instinctively that he could not produce aviators to meet the Western European; all his social instincts made him cling to the idea of a great motherly, almost sow-like bag of wind above him. At an enormous waste of resources Germany has produced these futile monsters, that drift in the darkness over England promiscuously dropping bombs on fields and houses. They are now meeting the fate that was demonstrably certain ten years ago. If they found us unready for them it is merely that we were unable to imagine so idiotic an enterprise would ever be seriously sustained and persisted in. We did not believe in the probability of Zeppelin raids any more than we believed that Germany would force the world into war. It was a thing too silly to be believed. But they came—to their certain fate. In the month after I returned from France and Italy, no less than four of these fatuities were exploded and destroyed within thirty miles of my Essex home.... There in chosen phrases you have the truth about these things. But now mark the perversion of thought due to spectacular effect.

I find over the Essex countryside, which has been for more than a year and a half a highway for Zeppelins, a new and curious admiration for them that has arisen out of these very disasters. Previously they were regarded with dislike and a sort of distrust, as one might regard a sneaking neighbour who left his footsteps in one's garden at night. But the Zeppelins of Billericay and Potter's Bar are—heroic things. (The Cuffley one came down too quickly, and the fourth one which came down for its crew to surrender is despised.) I have heard people describe the two former with eyes shining with enthusiasm.

"First," they say, "you saw a little round red glow that spread. Then you saw the whole Zeppelin glowing. Oh, it was *beautiful!* Then it began to turn over and come down, and it flames and pieces began to break away. And then down it came, leaving flaming pieces all up the sky. At last it was a pillar of fire eight thousand feet high.... Everyone said, 'Ooooo!' And then someone pointed out the little aeroplane lit up by the flare—such a leetle thing up there in the night! It is the greatest thing I have ever seen. Oh! the most wonderful—most wonderful!"

There is a feeling that the Germans really must after all be a splendid people to provide such magnificent pyrotechnics.

Some people in London the other day were pretending to be shocked by an American who boasted that he had been in "two *bully* bombardments," but he was only saying what everyone feels more or less. We are at a spectacle that—as a spectacle—our grandchildren will envy. I understand now better the story of the man who stared at the sparks raining up from his own house as it burnt in the night and whispered "*Lovely! Lovely!*"

The spectacular side of the war is really an enormous distraction from thought. And against thought there also fights the native indolence of the human mind. The human mind, it seems, was originally developed to think about the individual; it thinks reluctantly about the species. It takes refuge from that sort of thing if it possibly can. And so the second great preventive of clear thinking is the tranquillising platitude.

The human mind is an instrument very easily fatigued. Only a few exceptions go on thinking restlessly—to the extreme exasperation of their neighbours. The normal mind craves for decisions, even wrong or false decisions rather than none. It clutches at comforting falsehoods. It loves to be told, "*There*, don't you worry. That'll be all right. That's *settled*." This war has come as an almost overwhelming challenge to mankind. To some of us it seems as it if were the Sphynx proffering the alternative of its riddle or death. Yet the very urgency of this challenge to think seems to paralyse the critical intelligence of very many people altogether. They will say, "This war is going to produce enormous changes in everything." They will then subside mentally with a feeling of having covered the whole ground in a thoroughly safe manner. Or they will adopt an air of critical aloofness. They will say, "How is it possible to foretell what may happen in this tremendous sea of change?" And then, with an air of superior modesty, they will go on doing—whatever they feel inclined to do. Many others, a degree less simple in their methods, will take some entirely partial aspect, arrive at some guesswork decision upon that, and then behave as though that met every question we have to face. Or they will make a sort of admonitory forecast that is conditional upon the good behaviour of other people. "Unless the Trade Unions are more reasonable," they will say. Or, "Unless the shipping interest is grappled with and controlled." Or, "Unless England wakes up." And with that they seem to wash their hands of further responsibility for the future.

One delightful form of put-off is the sage remark, "Let us finish the war first, and then let us ask what is going to happen after it." One likes to think of the beautiful blank day after the signing of the peace when these wise minds swing round to pick up their deferred problems....

I submit that a man has not done his duty by himself as a rational creature unless he has formed an idea of what is going on, as one complicated process, until he has formed an idea sufficiently definite for him to make it the basis of a further idea, which is his own relationship to that process. He must have some notion of what the process is going to do to him, and some notion of what he means to do, if he can, to the process. That is to say, he must not only have an idea how the process is going, but also an idea of how he wants it to go. It seems so natural and necessary for a human brain to do this that it is hard to suppose that everyone has not more or less attempted it. But few people, in Great Britain at any rate, have the habit of frank expression, and when people do not seem to have made out any of these things for themselves there is a considerable element of secretiveness and inexpressiveness to be allowed for before we decide that they have not in some sort of fashion done so. Still, after all allowances have been made, there remains a vast amount of jerry-built and ready-made borrowed stuff in most of people's philosophies of the war. The systems of authentic opinion in this world of thought about the war are like comparatively rare thin veins of living mentality in a vast world of dead repetitions and echoed suggestions. And that being the case, it is quite possible that history after the war, like history before the war, will not be so much a display of human will and purpose as a resultant of human vacillations, obstructions, and inadvertences. We shall still be in a drama of blind forces following the line of least resistance.

One of the people who is often spoken of as if he were doing an enormous amount of concentrated thinking is "the man in the trenches." We are told—by gentlemen writing for the most part at home—of the most extraordinary things that are going on in those devoted brains, how they are getting new views about the duties of labour, religion, morality, monarchy, and any other notions that the gentleman at home happens to fancy and wished to push. Now that is not at all the impression of the khaki mentality I have reluctantly accepted as correct. For the most part the man in khaki is up against a round of tedious immediate duties that forbid consecutive thought; he is usually rather crowded and not very comfortable. He is bored.

The real horror of modern war, when all is said and done, is the boredom. To get killed our wounded may be unpleasant, but it is at any rate interesting; the real tragedy is in the desolated fields, the desolated houses, the desolated hours and days, the bored and desolated minds that hang behind the melee and just outside the melee. The peculiar beastliness of the German crime is the way the German war cant and its consequences have seized upon and paralysed the mental movement of Western Europe. Before 1914 war was theoretically unpopular in every European country; we thought of it as something tragic and dreadful. Now everyone knows by experience that it is something utterly dirty and detestable. We thought it was the Nemean lion, and we have found it is the Augean stable. But being bored by war and hating war is quite unproductive *unless you are thinking about its nature and causes so thoroughly that you will presently be able to take hold of it and control it and end it.* It is no good for everyone to say unanimously, "We will have no more war," unless you have thought out how to avoid it, and mean to bring that end about. It is as if everyone said, "We will have no more catarrh," or "no more flies," or "no more east wind." And my point is that the immense sorrows at home in every European country and the vast boredom of the combatants are probably not really producing any effective remedial mental action at all, and will not do so unless we get much more thoroughly to work upon the thinking-out process.

In such talks as I could get with men close up to the front I found beyond this great boredom and attempts at distraction only very specialised talk about changes in the future. Men were keen upon questions of army promotion, of the future of conscription, of the future of the temporary officer, upon the education of boys in relation to army needs. But the war itself was bearing them all upon its way, as unquestioned and uncontrolled as if it were the planet on which they lived.

II. THE YIELDING PACIFIST AND THE CONSCIENTIOUS OBJECTOR

1 Among the minor topics that people are talking about behind the western fronts is the psychology of the Yielding Pacifist and the Conscientious Objector. Of course, we are all pacifists nowadays; I know of no one who does not want not only to end this war but to put an end to war altogether, except those blood-red terrors Count Reventlow, Mr. Leo Maxse—how he does it on a vegetarian dietary I cannot imagine!—and our wild-eyed desperados of *The Morning Post*. But most of the people I meet, and most of the people I met on my journey, are pacifists like myself who want to *make* peace by beating the armed man until he gives in and admits the error of his ways, disarming him and reorganising the world for the forcible suppression of military adventures in the future. They want belligerency put into the same category as burglary, as a matter of forcible suppression. The Yielding Pacifist who will accept any sort of peace, and the Conscientious Objector who will not fight at all, are not of that opinion.

Both Italy and France produce parallel types to those latter, but it would seem that in each case England displays the finer developments. The Latin mind is directer than the English, and its standards—shall I say?—more primitive; it gets more directly to the fact that here are men who will not fight. And it is less charitable. I was asked quite a number of times for the English equivalent of an *embusque*. "We don't generalise," I said, "we treat each case on its merits!"

One interlocutor near Udine was exercised by our Italian Red Cross work.

"Here," he said, "are sixty or seventy young Englishmen, all fit for military service.... Of course they go under fire, but it is not like being junior officers in the trenches. Not one of them has been killed or wounded."

He reflected. "One, I think, has been decorated," he said....

My French and Italian are only for very rough common jobs; when it came to explaining the Conscientious Objector sympathetically they broke down badly. I had to construct long parenthetical explanations of our antiquated legislative methods to show how it was that the "conscientious objector" had been so badly defined. The foreigner does not understand the importance of vague definition in British life. "Practically, of course, we offered to exempt anyone who conscientiously objected to fight or serve. Then the Pacifist and German people started a campaign to enrol objectors.

Of course every shirker, every coward and slacker in the country decided at once to be a conscientious objector. Anyone but a British legislator could have foreseen that. Then we started Tribunals to wrangle with the objectors about their *bona fides*. Then the Pacifists and the Pro-Germans issued little leaflets and started correspondence courses to teach people exactly how to lie to the Tribunals. Trouble about freedom of the pamphleteer followed. I had to admit—it has been rather a sloppy business. The people who made the law knew their own minds, but we English are not an expressive people."

These are not easy things to say in Elementary (and slightly Decayed) French or in Elementary and Corrupt Italian.

"But why do people support the sham conscientious objector and issue leaflets to help him—when there is so much big work clamouring to be done?"

"That," I said, "is the Whig tradition."

When they pressed me further, I said: "I am really the questioner. I am visiting *your* country, and you have to tell *me* things. It is not right that I should do all the telling. Tell me all about Romain Rolland."

And so I pressed them about the official socialists in Italy and the Socialist minority in France until I got the question out of the net of national comparisons and upon a broader footing. In several conversations we began to work out in general terms the psychology of those people who were against the war. But usually we could not get to that; my interlocutors would insist upon telling me just what they would like to do or just what they would like to see done to stop-the-war pacifists and conscientious objectors; pleasant rather than fruitful imaginative exercises from which I could effect no more than platitudinous uplifts.

But the general drift of such talks as did seem to penetrate the question was this, that among these stop-the-war people there are really three types. First there is a type of person who hates violence and the infliction of pain under any circumstances, and who have a mystical belief in the rightness (and usually the efficacy) of non-resistance. These are generally Christians, and then their cardinal text is the instruction to "turn the other cheek." Often they are Quakers. If they are consistent they are vegetarians and wear *Lederlos* boots. They do not desire police protection for their goods. They stand aloof from all the force and conflict of life. They have always done so. This is an understandable and respectable type. It has numerous Hindu equivalents. It is a type that finds little difficulty about exemptions—provided the individual has not been too recently converted to his present habits. But it is not the prevalent type in stop-the-war circles. Such genuine ascetics do not number more than a thousand or so, all three of our western allied countries. The mass of the stop-the-war people is made up quite other elements.

2

In the complex structure of the modern community there are two groups or strata or pockets in which the impulse of social obligation, the gregarious sense of a common welfare, is at its lowest; one of these is the class of the Resentful Employee, the class of people who, without explanation, adequate preparation or any chance, have been shoved at an early age into uncongenial work and never given a chance to escape, and the other is the class of people with small fixed incomes or with small salaries earnt by routine work, or half independent people practising some minor artistic or literary craft, who have led uneventful, irresponsible lives from their youth up, and never came at any point into relations of service to the state. This latter class was more difficult to define than the former—because it is more various within itself. My French friends wanted to talk of the "Psychology of the Rentier." I was for such untranslatable phrases as the "Genteel Whig," or the "Donnish Liberal." But I lit up an Italian—he is a Milanese manufacturer—with "these Florentine English who would keep Italy in a glass case." "I know," he said. Before I go on to expand this congenial theme, let me deal first with the Resentful Employee, who is a much more considerable, and to me a much more sympathetic, figure in European affairs. I began life myself as a Resentful Employee. By the extremest good luck I have got my mind and spirit out of the distortions of that cramping beginning, but I can still recall even the anger of those old days.

He becomes an employee between thirteen and fifteen; he is made to do work he does not like for no other purpose that he can see except the profit and glory of a fortunate person called his employer, behind whom stand church and state blessing and upholding the relationship. He is not allowed to feel that he has any share whatever in the employer's business, or that any end is served but the employer's profit. He cannot see that the employer acknowledges any duty to the state. Neither church nor state seems to insist that the employer has any public function. At no point does the employee come into a clear relationship of mutual obligation with the state. There does not seem to be any way out for the employee from a life spent in this subordinate, toilsome relationship. He feels put upon and cheated out of life. He is without honour. If he is a person of ability or stubborn temper he struggles out of his position; if he is a kindly and generous person he blames his "luck" and does his work and lives his life as cheerfully as possible—and so live the bulk of our amazing European workers; if he is a being of great magnanimity he is content to serve for the ultimate good of the race; if he has imagination, he says, "Things will not always be like this," and becomes a socialist or a guild socialist, and tries to educate the employer to a sense of reciprocal duty; but if he is too human for any of these things, then he begins to despise and hate the employer and the system that made him. He wants to hurt them. Upon that hate it is easy to trade.

A certain section of what is called the Socialist press and the Socialist literature in Europe is no doubt great-minded; it seeks to carve a better world out of the present. But much of it is socialist only in name. Its spirit is Anarchistic. Its real burthen is not construction but grievance; it tells the bitter tale of the employee, it feeds and organises his malice, it schemes annoyance and injury for the hated employer. The state and the order of the world is confounded with the capitalist. Before the war the popular so-called socialist press reeked with the cant of rebellion, the cant of any sort of rebellion. "I'm a rebel," was the silly boast of the young disciple. "Spoil something, set fire to something," was held to be the proper text for any girl or lad of spirit. And this blind discontent carried on into the war. While on the one hand a great rush of men poured into the army saying, "Thank God! we can serve our country at last instead of some beastly profiteer," a sourer remnant, blind to the greater issues of the war, clung to the reasonless proposition, "the state is only for the Capitalist. This war is got up by Capitalists. Whatever has to be done—*we are rebels.*"

Such a typical paper as the British *Labour Leader*, for example, may be read in vain, number after number, for any sound and sincere constructive proposal. It is a prolonged scream of extreme individualism, a monotonous repetition of incoherent discontent with authority, with direction, with union, with the European effort. It wants to do nothing. It just wants effort to stop—even at the price of German victory. If the whole fabric of society in western Europe were to be handed over to those pseudo-socialists to-morrow, to be administered for the common good, they would fly the task in terror. They would make excuses and refuse the undertaking. They do not want the world to go right. The very idea of the world going right does not exist in their minds. They are embodied discontent and hatred, making trouble, and that is all they are. They want to be "rebels"—to be admired as "rebels".

That is the true psychology of the Resentful Employee. He is a de-socialised man. His sense of the State has been destroyed.

The Resentful Employees are the outcome of our social injustices. They are the failures of our social ad educational systems. We may regret their pitiful degradation, we may exonerate them from blame; none the less they are a pitiful crew. I have seen the hardship of the trenches, the gay and gallant wounded. I do a little understand what our soldiers, officers and men alike, have endured and done. And though I know I ought to allow for all that I have stated, I cannot regard these conscientious objectors with anything but contempt. Into my house there pours a dismal literature rehearsing the hardships of these men who set themselves up to be martyrs for liberty; So and So, brave hero, has been sworn at—positively sworn at by a corporal; a nasty rough man came into the cell of So and So and dropped several h's; So and So, refusing to undress and wash, has been undressed and washed, and soap was rubbed into his eyes—perhaps purposely; the food and accommodation are not of the best class; the doctors in attendance seem hasty; So and So was put into a damp bed and has got a nasty cold. Then I recall a jolly vanload of wounded men I saw out there....

But after all, we must be just. A church and state that permitted these people to be thrust into dreary employment in their early 'teens, without hope or pride, deserves such citizens as these. The marvel is that there are so few. There are a poor thousand or so of these hopeless, resentment-poisoned creatures in Great Britain. Against five willing millions. The Allied countries, I submit, have not got nearly all the conscientious objectors they deserve.

3

If the Resentful Employee provides the emotional impulse of the resisting pacifist, whose horizon is bounded by his one passionate desire that the particular social system that has treated him so ill should collapse and give in, and its leaders and rulers be humiliated and destroyed, the intellectual direction of a mischievous pacifism comes from an entirely different class.

The Genteel Whig, though he differs very widely in almost every other respect from the Resentful Employee, has this much in common, that he has never been drawn into the whirl of collective life in any real and assimilative fashion. This is what is the matter with both of them. He is a little loose, shy, independent person. Except for eating and drinking—in moderation, he has never done anything real from the day he was born. He has frequently not even faced the common challenge of matrimony. Still more frequently is he childless, or the daring parent of one particular child. He has never traded nor manufactured. He has drawn his dividends or his salary with an entire unconsciousness of any obligations to policemen or navy for these punctual payments. Probably he has never ventured even to reinvest his little legacy. He is acutely aware of possessing an exceptionally fine intelligence, but he is entirely unconscious of a fundamental unreality. Nothing has ever occurred to him to make him ask why the mass of men were either not possessed of his security or discontented with it. The impulses that took his school friends out upon all sorts of odd feats and adventures struck him as needless. As he grew up he turned with an equal distrust from passion or ambition. His friends went out after love, after adventure, after power, after knowledge, after this or that desire, and became men. But he noted merely that they became fleshly, that effort strained them, that they were sometimes angry or violent or heated. He could not but feel that theirs were vulgar experiences, and he sought some finer exercise for his exceptional quality. He pursued art or philosophy or literature upon their more esoteric levels, and realised more and more the general vulgarity and coarseness of the world about him, and his own detachment. The vulgarity and crudity of the things nearest him impressed him most; the dreadful insincerity of the Press, the meretriciousness of success, the loudness of the rich, the baseness of common people in his own land. The world overseas had by comparison a certain glamour. Except that when you said "United States" to him he would draw the air sharply between his teeth and beg you not to...

Nobody took him by the collar and shook him.

If our world had considered the advice of William James and insisted upon national service from everyone, national service in the drains or the nationalised mines or the nationalised deep-sea fisheries if not in the army or navy, we should not have had any such men. If it had insisted that wealth and property are no more than a trust for the public benefit, we should have had no genteel indispensables. These discords in our national unanimity are the direct consequence of our bad social organisation. We permit the profiteer and the usurer; they evoke the response of the Reluctant Employee, and the inheritor of their wealth becomes the Genteel Whig.

But that is by the way. It was of course natural and inevitable that the German onslaught upon Belgium and civilisation generally should strike these recluse minds not as a monstrous ugly wickedness to be resisted and overcome at any cost, but merely as a nerve-racking experience. Guns were going off on both sides. The Genteel Whig was chiefly conscious of a repulsive vast excitement all about him, in which many people did inelegant and irrational things. They waved flags—nasty little flags. This child of the ages, this last fruit of the gigantic and tragic tree of life, could no more than stick its fingers in its ears as say, "Oh, please, do *all* stop!" and then as the strain grew intenser and intenser set itself with feeble pawings now to clamber "Au-dessus de la Melee," and now to—in some weak way—stop the conflict. ("Au-dessus de la Melee"—as the man said when they asked him where he was when the bull gored his sister.) The efforts to stop the conflict at any price, even at the price of entire submission to the German

Will, grew more urgent as the necessity that everyone should help against the German Thing grew more manifest.

Of all the strange freaks of distressed thinking that this war has produced, the freaks of the Genteel Whig have been among the most remarkable. With an air of profound wisdom he returns perpetually to his proposition that there are faults on both sides. To say that is his conception of impartiality. I suppose that if a bull gored his sister he would say that there were faults on both sides; his sister ought not to have strayed into the field, she was wearing a red hat of a highly provocative type; she ought to have been a cow and then everything would have been different. In the face of the history of the last forty years, the Genteel Whig struggles persistently to minimise the German outrage upon civilisation and to find excuses for Germany. He does this, not because he has any real passion for falsehood, but because by training, circumstance, and disposition he is passionately averse from action with the vulgar majority and from self-sacrifice in a common cause, and because he finds in the justification of Germany and, failing that, in the blackening of the Allies to an equal blackness, one line of defence against the wave of impulse that threatens to submerge his private self. But when at last that line is forced he is driven back upon others equally extraordinary. You can often find simultaneously in the same Pacifist paper, and sometimes even in the utterances of the same writer, two entirely incompatible statements. The first is that Germany is so invincible that it is useless to prolong the war since no effort of the Allies is likely to produce any material improvement in their position, and the second is that Germany is so thoroughly beaten that she is now ready to abandon militarism and make terms and compensations entirely acceptable to the countries she has forced into war. And when finally facts are produced to establish the truth that Germany, though still largely wicked and impenitent, is being slowly and conclusively beaten by the sanity, courage and persistence of the Allied common men, then the Genteel Whig retorts with his last defensive absurdity. He invents a national psychology for Germany. Germany, he invents, loves us and wants to be our dearest friend. Germany has always loved us. The Germans are a loving, unenvious people. They have been a little mislead—but nice people do not insist upon that fact. But beware of beating Germany, beware of humiliating Germany; then indeed trouble will come. Germany will begin to dislike us. She will plan a revenge. Turning aside from her erstwhile innocent career, she may even think of hate. What are our obligations to France, Italy, Serbia and Russia, what is the happiness of a few thousands of the Herero, a few millions of the Belgians—whose numbers moreover are constantly diminishing—when we might weigh them against the danger, the most terrible danger, of incurring *permanent German hostility?*...

A Frenchman I talked to knew better than that. "What will happen to Germany," I asked, "if we are able to do so to her and so; would she take to dreams of a *Revanche?*"

"She will take to Anglomania," he said, and added after a flash of reflection, "In the long run it will be the worse for you."

III. THE RELIGIOUS REVIVAL

1

One of the indisputable things about the war, so far as Britain and France go—and I have reason to believe that on a lesser scale things are similar in Italy—is that it has produced a very great volume of religious thought and feeling. About Russia in these matters we hear but little at the present time, but one guesses at parallelism. People habitually religious have been stirred to new depths of reality and sincerity, and people are thinking of religion who never thought of religion before. But as I have already pointed out, thinking and feeling about a matter is of no permanent value unless something is *thought out*, unless there is a change of boundary or relationship, and it an altogether different question to ask whether any definite change is resulting from this universal ferment. If it is not doing so, then the sleeper merely dreams a dream that he will forget again....

Now in no sort of general popular mental activity is there so much froth and waste as in religious excitements. This has been the case in all periods of religious revival. The number who are rather impressed, who for a few days or weeks take to reading their Bibles or going to a new place of worship or praying or fasting or being kind and unselfish, is always enormous in relation to the people whose lives are permanently changed. The effort needed if a contemporary is to blow off the froth, is always very considerable.

Among the froth that I would blow off is I think most of the tremendous efforts being made in England by the Anglican church to attract favourable attention to itself *apropos* of the war. I came back from my visit to the Somme battlefields to find the sylvan peace of Essex invaded by a number of ladies in blue dresses adorned with large white crosses, who, regardless of the present shortage of nurses, were visiting every home in the place on some mission of invitation whose details remained obscure. So far as I was able to elucidate this project, it was in the nature of a magic incantation; a satisfactory end of the war was to be brought about by convergent prayer and religious assiduities. The mission was shy of dealing with me personally, although as a lapsed communicant I should have thought myself a particularly hopeful field for Anglican effort, and it came to my wife and myself merely for our permission and countenance in an appeal to our domestic servants. My wife consulted the household; it seemed very anxious to escape from that appeal, and as I respect Christianity sufficiently to detest the identification of its services with magic processes, the mission retired—civilly repulsed. But the incident aroused an uneasy curiosity in my mind with regard to the general trend of Anglican teaching and Anglican activities at the present time. The trend of my enquiries is to discover the church much more incoherent and much less religious—in any decent sense of the word—than I had supposed it to be.

Organisation is the life of material and the death of mental and spiritual processes. There could be no more melancholy exemplification of this than the spectacle of the Anglican and Catholic churches at the present time, one using the tragic stresses of war mainly for pew-rent touting, and the other paralysed by its Austrian and South German political connections from any clear utterance upon the moral issues of the war. Through the opening phases of the war the Established Church of England was inconspicuous; this is no longer the case, but it may be doubted whether the change is altogether to its advantage. To me this is a very great disappointment. I have always had a very high opinion of the intellectual values of the leading divines of both the Anglican and Catholic communions. The self-styled Intelligentsia of Great Britain is all too prone to sneer at their equipment; but I do not see how any impartial person can deny that Father Bernard Vaughn is in mental energy, vigour of expression, richness of thought and variety of information fully the equal of such an influential lay publicist as Mr. Horatio Bottomley. One might search for a long time among prominent laymen to find the equal of the Bishop of London. Nevertheless it is impossible to conceal the impression of tawdriness that this latter gentleman's work as head of the National Mission has left upon my mind. Attired in khaki he has recently been preaching in the open air to the people of London upon Tower Hill, Piccadilly, and other conspicuous places. Obsessed as I am by the humanities, and impressed as I have always been by the inferiority of material to moral facts, I would willingly have exchanged the sight of two burning Zeppelins for this spectacle of ecclesiastical fervour. But as it is, I am obliged to trust to newspaper reports and the descriptions of hearers and eye-witnesses. They leave to me but little doubt of the regrettable superficiality of the bishop's utterances.

We have a multitude of people chastened by losses, ennobled by a common effort, needing support in that effort, perplexed by the reality of evil and cruelty, questioning and seeking after God. What does the National Mission offer? On Tower Hill the bishop seems to have been chiefly busy with a wrangling demonstration that ten thousand a year is none too big a salary for a man subject to such demands and expenses as his see involves. So far from making anything out of his see he was, he declared, two thousand a year to the bad. Some day, when the church has studied efficiency, I suppose that bishops will have the leisure to learn something about the general state of opinion and education in their dioceses. The

Bishop of London was evidently unaware of the almost automatic response of the sharp socialists among his hearers. Their first enquiry would be to learn how he came by that mysterious extra two thousand a year with which he supplemented his stipend. How did he earn *that?* And if he didn't earn it——! And secondly, they would probably have pointed out to him that his standard of housing, clothing, diet and entertaining was probably a little higher than theirs. It is really no proof of virtuous purity that a man's expenditure exceeds his income. And finally some other of his hearers were left unsatisfied by his silence with regard to the current proposal to pool all clerical stipends for the common purposes of the church. It is a reasonable proposal, and if bishops must dispute about stipends instead of preaching the kingdom of God, then they are bound to face it. The sooner they do so, the more graceful will the act be. From these personal apologetics the bishop took up the question of the exemption, at the request of the bishops, of the clergy from military service. It is one of our contrasts with French conditions—and it is all to the disadvantage of the British churches.

In his Piccadilly contribution to the National Mission of Repentance and Hope the bishop did not talk politics but sex. He gave his hearers the sort of stuff that is handed out so freely by the Cinema Theatres, White Slave Traffic talk, denunciations of "Night Hawks"—whatever "Night Hawks" may be—and so on. One this or another occasion the bishop—he boasts that he himself is a healthy bachelor—lavished his eloquence upon the Fall in the Birth Rate, and the duty of all married people, from paupers upward, to have children persistently. Now sex, like diet, is a department of conduct and a very important department, but *it isn't religion!* The world is distressed by international disorder, by the monstrous tragedy of war; these little hot talks about indulgence and begetting have about as much to do with the vast issues that concern us as, let us say, a discussion of the wickedness of eating very new and indigestible bread. It is talking round and about the essential issue. It is fogging the essential issue, which is the forgotten and neglected kingship of God. The sin that is stirring the souls of men is the sin of this war. It is the sin of national egotism and the devotion of men to loyalties, ambitions, sects, churches, feuds, aggressions, and divisions that are an outrage upon God's universal kingdom.

2

The common clergy of France, sharing the military obligations and the food and privations of their fellow parishioners, contrast very vividly with the home-staying types of the ministries of the various British churches. I met and talked to several. Near Frise there were some barge gunboats— they have since taken their place in the fighting, but then they were a surprise—and the men had been very anxious to have their craft visited and seen. The priest who came after our party to see if he could still arrange that, had been decorated for gallantry. Of course the English too have their gallant chaplains, but they are men of the officer caste, they are just young officers with peculiar collars; not men among men, as are the French priests.

There can be no doubt that the behaviour of the French priests in this war has enormously diminished anti-clerical bitterness in France. There can be no doubt that France is far more a religious country than it was before the war. But if you ask whether that means any return to the church, any reinstatement of the church, the answer is a doubtful one. Religion and the simple priest are stronger in France to-day; the church, I think, is weaker.

I trench on no theological discussion when I record the unfavourable impression made upon all western Europe by the failure of the Holy Father to pronounce definitely upon the rights and wrongs of the war. The church has abrogated its right of moral judgement. Such at least seemed to be the opinion of the Frenchmen with whom I discussed a remarkable interview with Cardinal Gasparri that I found one morning in *Le Journal.*

It was not the sort of interview to win the hearts of men who were ready to give their lives to set right what they believe to be the greatest outrage that has ever been inflicted upon Christendom, that is to say the forty-three years of military preparation and of diplomacy by threats that culminated in the ultimatum to Serbia, the invasion of Belgium and the murder of the Vise villagers. It was adorned with a large portrait of "Benoit XV.," looking grave and discouraging over his spectacles, and the headlines insisted it was "*La Pensee du Pape*." Cross-heads sufficiently indicated the general tone. One read:

"*Le Saint Siege impartial... Au-dessus de la bataille....*" The good Cardinal would have made a good lawyer. He had as little to say about God and the general righteousness of things as the Bishop of London. But he got in some smug reminders of the severance of diplomatic relations with the Vatican. Perhaps now France will be wiser. He pointed out that the Holy See in its Consistorial Allocution of January 22nd, 1915, invited the belligerents to observe the rules of war. Could anything more be done than that? Oh!—in the general issue of the war, if you want a judgement on the war as a whole, how is it possible that the Vatican to decide? Surely the French know that excellent principle of justice, *Audiatur et altera pars*, and how under existing circumstances can the Vatican do that...? The Vatican is cut off from communication with Austria and Germany. The Vatican has been deprived of its temporal power and local independence (another neat point)....

So France is bowed out. When peace is restored, the Vatican will perhaps be able to enquire if there was a big German army in 1914, if

German diplomacy was aggressive from 1875 onward, if Belgium was invaded unrighteously, if (Catholic) Austria forced the pace upon (non-Catholic) Russia. But now—now the Holy See must remain as impartial as an unbought mascot in a shop window....

The next column of *Le Journal* contained an account of the Armenian massacres; the blood of the Armenian cries out past the Holy Father to heaven; but then Armenians are after all heretics, and here again the principle of *Audiatur et altera pars* comes in. Communications are not open with the Turks. Moreover, Armenians, like Serbs, are worse than infidels; they are heretics. Perhaps God is punishing them....

Audiatur et altera pars, and the Vatican has not forgotten the infidelity and disrespect of both France and Italy in the past. These are the things, it seems, that really matter to the Vatican. Cardinal Gasparri's portrait, in the same issue of *Le Journal*, displays a countenance of serene contentment, a sort of incarnate "Told-you-so."

So the Vatican lifts its pontifical skirts and shakes the dust of western Europe off its feet.

It is the most astounding renunciation in history.

Indubitably the Christian church took a wide stride from the kingship of God when it placed a golden throne for the unbaptised Constantine in the midst of its most sacred deliberations at Nicaea. But it seems to me that this abandonment of moral judgements in the present case by the Holy See is an almost wider step from the church's allegiance to God....

3

Thought about the great questions of life, thought and reasoned direction, this is what the multitude demands mutely and weakly, and what the organised churches are failing to give. They have not the courage of their creeds. Either their creeds are intellectual flummery or they are the solution to the riddles with which the world is struggling. But the churches make no mention of their creeds. They chatter about sex and the magic effect of church attendance and simple faith. If simple faith is enough, the churches and their differences are an imposture. Men are stirred to the deepest questions about life and God, and the Anglican church, for example, obliges—as I have described.

It is necessary to struggle against the unfavourable impression made by these things. They must not blind us to the deeper movement that is in progress in a quite considerable number of minds in England and France alike towards the realisation of the kingdom of God.

What I conceive to be the reality of the religious revival is to be found in quarters remote from the religious professionals. Let me give but one instance of several that occur to me. I met soon after my return from France a man who has stirred my curiosity for years, Mr. David Lubin, the prime mover in the organisation of the International Institute of Agriculture in Rome. It is a movement that has always appealed to my imagination. The idea is to establish and keep up to date a record of the food supplies in the world with a view to the ultimate world control of food supply and distribution. When its machinery has developed sufficiently to a control in the interests of civilisation of many other staples besides foodstuffs. It is in fact the suggestion and beginning of the economic world peace and the economic world state, just as the Hague Tribunal is the first faint sketch of a legal world state. The King of Italy has met Mr. Lubin's idea with open hands. (It was because of this profoundly interesting experiment that in a not very widely known book of mine, *The World Set Free* (May, 1914), in which I represented a world state as arising out of Armageddon, I made the first world conference meet at Brissago in Italian Switzerland under the presidency of the King of Italy.) So that when I found I could meet Mr. Lubin I did so very gladly. We lunched together in a pretty little room high over Knightsbridge, and talked through an afternoon.

He is a man rather after the type of Gladstone; he could be made to look like Gladstone in a caricature, and he has that compelling quality of intense intellectual excitement which was one of the great factors in the personal effectiveness of Gladstone. He is a Jew, but until I had talked to him for some time that fact did not occur to me. He is in very ill health, he has some weakness of the heart that grips him and holds him at times white and silent.

At first we talked of his Institute and its work. Then we came to shipping and transport. Whenever one talks now of human affairs one comes presently to shipping and transport generally. In Paris, in Italy, when I returned to England, everywhere I found "cost of carriage" was being discovered to be a question of fundamental importance. Yet transport, railroads and shipping, these vitally important services in the world's affairs, are nearly everywhere in private hands and run for profit. In the case of shipping they are run for profit on such antiquated lines that freights vary from day to day and from hour to hour. It makes the business of food supply a gamble. And it need not be a gamble.

But that is by the way in the present discussion. As we talked, the prospect broadened out from a prospect of the growing and distribution of food to a general view of the world becoming one economic community.

I talked of various people I had been meeting in the previous few weeks. "So many of us," I said, "seem to be drifting away from the ideas of nationalism and faction and policy, towards something else which is larger. It is an idea of a right way of doing things for human purposes, independently of these limited and localised references. Take such things as international hygiene for example, take *this* movement. We are feeling our way towards a bigger rule."

"The rule of Righteousness," said Mr. Lubin.

I told him that I had been coming more and more to the idea—not as a sentimentality or a metaphor, but as the ruling and directing idea, the structural idea, of all one's political and social activities—of the whole world as one state and community and of God as the King of that state.

"But *I* say that," cried Mr. Lubin, "I have put my name to that. And—it is *here!*"

He struggled up, seized an Old Testament that lay upon a side table. He stood over it and rapped its cover. "It is *here*," he said, looking more like Gladstone than ever, "in the Prophets."

4

That is all I mean to tell at present of that conversation.

We talked of religion for two hours. Mr. Lubin sees things in terms of Israel and I do not. For all that we see things very much after the same fashion. That talk was only one of a number of talks about religion that I have had with hard and practical men who want to get the world straighter than it is, and who perceive that they must have a leadership and reference outside themselves. That is why I assert so confidently that there is a real deep religious movement afoot in the world. But not one of those conversations could have gone on, it would have ceased instantly, if anyone bearing the uniform and brand of any organised religious body, any clergyman, priest, mollah, of suchlike advocate of the ten thousand patented religions in the world, had come in. He would have brought in his sectarian spites, his propaganda of church-going, his persecution of the heretic and the illegitimate, his ecclesiastical politics, his taboos, and his doctrinal touchiness.... That is why, though I perceive there is a great wave of religious revival in the world to-day, I doubt whether it bodes well for the professional religions....

The other day I was talking to an eminent Anglican among various other people and someone with an eye to him propounded this remarkable view.

"There are four stages between belief and utter unbelief. There are those who believe in God, those who doubt like Huxley the Agnostic, those who deny him like the Atheists but who do at least keep his place vacant, and lastly those who have set up a Church in his place. That is the last outrage of unbelief."

IV. THE RIDDLE OF THE BRITISH

All the French people I met in France seemed to be thinking and talking about the English. The English bring their own atmosphere with them; to begin with they are not so talkative, and I did not find among them anything like the same vigour of examination, the same resolve to understand the Anglo-French reaction, that I found among the French. In intellectual processes I will confess that my sympathies are undisguisedly with the French; the English will never think nor talk clearly until the get clerical "Greek" and sham "humanities" out of their public schools and sincere study and genuine humanities in; our disingenuous Anglican compromise is like a cold in the English head, and the higher education in England is a training in evasion. This is an always lamentable state of affairs, but just now it is particularly lamentable because quite tremendous opportunities for the good of mankind turn on the possibility of a thorough and entirely frank mutual understanding between French, Italians, and English. For years there has been a considerable amount of systematic study in France of English thought and English developments. Upon almost any question of current English opinion and upon most current English social questions, the best studies are in French. But there has been little or no reciprocal activity. The English in France seem to confine their French studies to *La Vie Parisienne*. It is what they have been led to expect of French literature.

There can be no doubt in any reasonable mind that this war is binding France and England very closely together. They dare not quarrel for the next fifty years. They are bound to play a central part in the World League for the Preservation of Peace that must follow this struggle. There is no question of their practical union. It is a thing that must be. But it is remarkable that while the French mind is agog to apprehend every fact and detail it can about the British, to make the wisest and fullest use of our binding necessities, that strange English "incuria"—to use the new slang—attains to its most monumental in this matter.

So there is not much to say about how the British think about the French. They do not think. They feel. At the outbreak of the war, when the performance of France seemed doubtful, there was an enormous feeling for France in Great Britain; it was like the formless feeling one has for a brother. It was as if Britain had discovered a new instinct. If France had crumpled up like paper, the English would have fought on passionately to restore her. That is ancient history now. Now the English still feel fraternal and fraternally proud; but in a mute way they are dazzled. Since the

German attack on Verdun began, the French have achieved a crescendo. None of us could have imagined it. It did not seem possible to very many of us at the end of 1915 that either France or Germany could hold on for another year. There was much secret anxiety for France. It has given place now to unstinted confidence and admiration. In their astonishment the British are apt to forget the impressive magnitude of their own effort, the millions of soldiers, the innumerable guns, the endless torrent of supplies that pour into France to avenge the little army of Mons. It seems natural to us that we should so exert ourselves under the circumstances. I suppose it is wonderful, but, as a sample Englishman, I do not feel that it is at all wonderful. I did not feel it wonderful even when I saw the British aeroplanes lording it in the air over Martinpuich, and not a German to be seen. Since Michael would have it so, there, at last, they were.

There was a good deal of doubt in France about the vigour of the British effort, until the Somme offensive. All that had been dispelled in August when I reached Paris. There was not the shadow of a doubt remaining anywhere of the power and loyalty of the British. These preliminary assurances have to be made, because it is in the nature of the French mind to criticise, and it must not be supposed that criticisms of detail and method affect the fraternity and complete mutual confidence which is the stuff of the Anglo-French relationship.

2

Now first the French have been enormously astonished by the quality of the ordinary British soldiers in our new armies. One Colonial colonel said something almost incredible to me—almost incredible as coming as from a Frenchman; it was a matter to solemn for any compliments or polite exaggerations; he said in tones of wonder and conviction, "*They are as good as ours.*" It was his acme of all possible praise.

That means any sort of British soldier. Unless he is assisted by a kilt the ordinary Frenchman is unable to distinguish between one sort of British soldier and another. He cannot tell—let the ardent nationalist mark the fact!—a Cockney from an Irishman or the Cardiff from the Essex note. He finds them all extravagantly and unquenchably cheerful and with a generosity—"like good children." There his praise is a little tinged by doubt. The British are reckless—recklessness in battle a Frenchman can understand, but they are also reckless about to-morrow's bread and whether the tent is safe against a hurricane in the night. He is struck too by the fact that they are much more vocal than the French troops, and that they seem to have a passion for bad lugubrious songs. There he smiles and shrugs his shoulders, and indeed what else can any of us do in the presence of that mystery? At any rate the legend of the "phlegmatic" Englishman has been scattered to the four winds of heaven by the guns of the western front. The men are cool in action, it is true; but for the rest they are, by the French standards, quicksilver.

But I will not expand further upon the general impression made by the English in France. Philippe Millet's *En Liaison avec les Anglais* gives in a series of delightful pictures portraits of British types from the French angle. There can be little doubt that the British quality, genial naive, plucky and generous, has won for itself a real affection in France wherever it has had a chance to display itself....

But when it comes to British methods then the polite Frenchman's difficulties begin. Translating hints into statements and guessing at reservations, I would say that the French fall very short of admiration of the way in which our higher officers set about their work, they are disagreeably impressed by a general want of sedulousness and close method in our leading. They think we economise brains and waste blood. They are shocked at the way in which obviously incompetent or inefficient men of the old army class are retained in their positions even after serious failures, and they were profoundly moved by the bad staff work and needlessly heavy losses of our opening attacks in July. They were ready to condone the blunderings and flounderings of the 1915 offensive as the necessary penalties of an "amateur" army, they had had to learn their own lesson in Champagne, but they were surprised to find how much the British had still to learn in July, 1916. The British officers excuse themselves because, they plead, they are still amateurs. "That is no reason," says the Frenchman, "why they should be amateurish."

No Frenchman said as much as this to me, but their meaning was as plain as daylight. I tackled one of my guides on this matter; I said that it was the plain duty of the French military people to criticise British military methods sharply if they thought they were wrong. "It is not easy," he said. "Many British officers do not think they have anything to learn. And English people do not like being told things. What could we do? We could hardly send a French officer or so to your headquarters in a tutorial capacity. You have to do things in your own way." When I tried to draw General Castelnau into this dangerous question by suggesting that we might borrow a French general or so, he would say only, "There is only one way to learn war, and that is to make war." When it was too late, in the lift, I thought of the answer to that. There is only one way to make war, and that is by the sacrifice of incapables and the rapid promotion of able men. If old and tried types fail now, new types must be sought. But to do that we want a standard of efficiency. We want a conception of intellectual quality in performance that is still lacking....

M. Joseph Reinach, in whose company I visited the French part of the Somme front, was full of a scheme, which he has since published, for the breaking up and recomposition of the French and British armies into a series of composite armies which would blend the magnificent British manhood and material with French science and military experience. He pointed out the endless advantages of such an arrangement; the stimulus of emulation, the promotion of intimate fraternal feeling between the peoples of the two countries. "At present," he said, "no Frenchman ever sees an Englishman except at Amiens or on the Somme. Many of them still have no idea of what the English are doing...."

"Have I ever told you the story of compulsory Greek at Oxford and Cambridge?" I asked abruptly.

"What has that to do with it?"

"Or how two undistinguished civil service commissioners can hold up the scientific education of our entire administrative class?"

M. Reinach protested further.

"Because you are proposing to loosen the grip of a certain narrow and limited class upon British affairs, and you propose it as though it were a job as easy as rearranging railway fares or sending a van to Calais. That is the problem that every decent Englishman is trying to solve to-day, every man of that Greater Britain which has supplied these five million volunteers, these magnificent temporary officers and all this wealth of munitions. And the oligarchy is so invincibly fortified! Do you think it will let in Frenchmen to share its controls? It will not even let in Englishmen. It holds the class schools; the class universities; the examinations for our public services are its class shibboleths; it is the church, the squirearchy, the permanent army class, permanent officialdom; it makes every appointment, it is the fountain of honour; what it does not know is not knowledge, what it cannot do must not be done. It rules India ignorantly and obstructively; it will wreck the empire rather than relinquish its ascendancy in Ireland. It is densely self-satisfied and instinctively monopolistic. It is on our backs, and with it on our backs we common English must bleed and blunder to victory.... And you make this proposal!"

3

The antagonistic relations of the Anglican oligarchy with the greater and greater-spirited Britain that thrust behind it in this war are probably paralleled very closely in Germany, probably they are exaggerated in Germany with a bigger military oligarchy and a relatively lesser civil body under it. This antagonism is the oddest outcome of the tremendous *de-militarisation* of war that has been going on. In France it is probably not so marked because of the greater flexibility and adaptability of the French culture.

All military people—people, that is, professionally and primarily military—are inclined to be conservative. For thousands of years the military tradition has been a tradition of discipline. The conception of the common soldier has been a mechanically obedient, almost dehumanised man, of the of officer a highly trained autocrat. In two years all this has been absolutely reversed. Individual quality, inventive organisation and industrialism will win this war. And no class is so innocent of these things as the military caste. Long accustomed as they are to the importance of moral effect they put a brave face upon the business; they save their faces astonishingly, but they are no longer guiding and directing this war, they are being pushed from behind by forces they never foresaw and cannot control. The aeroplanes and great guns have bolted with them, the tanks begotten of naval and civilian wits, shove them to victory in spite of themselves.

Wherever I went behind the British lines the officers were going about in spurs. These spurs at last got on my nerves. They became symbolical. They became as grave an insult to the tragedy of the war as if they were false noses. The British officers go for long automobile rides in spurs. They walk about the trenches in spurs. Occasionally I would see a horse; I do not wish to be unfair in this matter, there were riding horses sometimes within two or three miles of the ultimate front, but they were rarely used.

I do not say that the horse is entirely obsolescent in this war. In was nothing is obsolete. In the trenches men fight with sticks. In the Pasubio battle the other day one of the Alpini silenced a machine gun by throwing stones. In the West African campaign we have employed troops armed with bows and arrows, and they have done very valuable work. But these are exceptional cases. The military use of the horse henceforth will be such an exceptional case. It is ridiculous for these spurs still to clink about the modern battlefield. What the gross cost of the spurs and horses and trappings of the British army amount to, and how many men are grooming and tending horses who might just as well be ploughing and milking at home, I cannot guess; it must be a total so enormous as seriously to affect the balance of the war.

And these spurs and their retention are only the outward and visible symbol of the obstinate resistance of the Anglican intelligence to the clear logic of the present situation. It is not only the external equipment of our leaders that falls behind the times; our political and administrative services are in the hands of the same desolatingly inadaptable class. The British are still wearing spurs in Ireland; they are wearing them in India; and the age of the spur has passed. At the outset of this war there was an absolute cessation of criticism of the military and administrative castes; it is becoming a question whether we may not pay too heavily in blundering and waste, in military and economic lassitude, in international irritation and the accumulation of future dangers in Ireland, Egypt, India, and elsewhere, for an apparent absence of internal friction. These people have no gratitude for tacit help, no spirit of intelligent service, and no sense of fair play to the outsider. The latter deficiency indeed they call *esprit de corps* and prize it as if it were a noble quality.

It becomes more and more imperative that the foreign observer should distinguish between this narrower, older official Britain and the greater newer Britain that struggles to free itself from the entanglement of a system outgrown. There are many Englishmen who would like to say to the French and Irish and the Italians and India, who indeed feel every week now a more urgent need of saying, "Have patience with us." The Riddle of the British is very largely solved if you will think of a great modern liberal nation seeking to slough an exceedingly tough and tight skin....

Nothing is more illuminating and self-educational than to explain one's home politics to an intelligent foreigner enquirer; it strips off all the secondary considerations, the allusiveness, the merely tactical considerations, the allusiveness, the merely tactical considerations. One sees the forest not as a confusion of trees but as something with a definite shape and place. I was asked in Italy and in France, "Where does Lord Northcliffe come into the British system—or Lloyd George? Who is Mr. Redmond? Why is Lloyd George a Minister, and why does not Mr. Redmond take office? Isn't there something called an ordnance department, and why is there a separate ministry of munitions? Can Mr. Lloyd George remove an incapable general?..."

I found it M. Joseph Reinach particularly penetrating and persistent. It is an amusing but rather difficult exercise to recall what I tried to convey to him by way of a theory of Britain. He is by no means an uncritical listener. I explained that there is an "inner Britain," official Britain, which is Anglican or official Presbyterian, which at the outside in the whole world cannot claim to speak for twenty million Anglican or Presbyterian communicants, which monopolises official positions, administration and honours in the entire British empire, dominates the court, and, typically, is spurred and red-tabbed. (It was just at this time that the spurs were most on my nerves.)

This inner Britain, I went on to explain, holds tenaciously to its positions of advantage, from which it is difficult to dislodge it without upsetting the whole empire, and it insists upon treating the rest of the four hundred millions who constitute that empire as outsiders, foreigners, subject races and suspected persons.

"To you," I said, "it bears itself with an appearance of faintly hostile, faintly contemptuous apathy. It is still so entirely insular that it shudders at the thought of the Channel Tunnel. This is the Britain which irritates and puzzles you so intensely—that you are quite unable to conceal these feelings from me. Unhappily it is the Britain you see most of. Well, outside this official Britain is 'Greater Britain'—the real Britain with which you have to reckon in the future." (From this point a faint flavour of mysticism crept into my dissertation. I found myself talking with something in my voice curiously reminiscent of those liberal Russians who set themselves to explain the contrasts and contradictions of "official" Russia and "true" Russia.) "This Greater Britain," I asserted, "is in a perpetual conflict with official Britain, struggling to keep it up to its work, shoving it towards its ends, endeavouring in spite of its tenacious mischievousness of the privileged to keep the peace and a common aim with the French and Irish and Italians and Russians and Indians. It is to that outer Britain that those Englishmen you found so interesting and sympathetic, Lloyd George and Lord Northcliffe, for example, belong. It is the Britain of the great effort, the Britain of the smoking factories and the torrent of munitions, the Britain of the men and subalterns of the new armies, the Britain which invents and thinks and achieves, and stands now between German imperialism and the empire of the world. I do not want to exaggerate the quality of greater Britain. If the inner set are narrowly educated, the outer set if often crudely educated. If the inner set is so close knit as to seem like a conspiracy, the outer set is so loosely knit as to seem like a noisy confusion. Greater Britain is only beginning to realise itself and find itself. For all its crudity there is a giant spirit in it feeling its way towards the light. It has quite other ambitions for the ending of the war than some haggled treaty of alliance with France and Italy; some advantage that will invalidate German competition; it begins to realise newer and wider sympathies, possibilities of an amalgamation of interests and community of aim that is utterly beyond the habits of the old oligarchy to conceive, beyond the scope of that tawdry word 'Empire' to express...."

I descended from my rhetoric to find M. Reinach asking how and when this greater Britain was likely to become politically effective.

V. THE SOCIAL CHANGES IN PROGRESS

1

"Nothing will be the same after the war." This is one of the consoling platitudes with which people cover over voids of thought. They utter it with an air of round-eyed profundity. But to ask in reply, "Then how will things be different?" is in many cases to rouse great resentment. It is almost as rude as saying, "Was that thought of yours really a thought?"

Let us in this chapter confine ourselves to the social-economic processes that are going on. So far as I am able to distinguish among the things that are being said in these matters, they may be classified out into groups that centre upon several typical questions. There is the question of "How to pay for the war?" There is the question of the behaviour of labour after the war. "Will there be a Labour Truce or a violent labour struggle?" There is the question of the reconstruction of European industry after the war in the face of an America in a state of monetary and economic repletion through non-intervention. My present purpose in this chapter is a critical one; it is not to solve problems but to set out various currents of thought that are flowing through the general mind. Which current is likely to seize upon and carry human affairs with it, is not for our present speculation.

There seem to be two distinct ways of answering the first of the questions I have noted. They do not necessarily contradict each other. Of course the war is being largely paid for immediately out of the accumulated private wealth of the past. We are buying off the "hold-up" of the private owner upon the material and resources we need, and paying in paper money and war loans. This is not in itself an impoverishment of the community. The wealth of individuals is not the wealth of nations; the two things may easily be contradictory when the rich man's wealth consists of land or natural resources or franchises or privileges the use of which he reluctantly yields for high prices. The conversion of held-up land and material into workable and actively used material in exchange for national debt may be indeed a positive increase in the wealth of the community. And what is happening in all the belligerent countries is the taking over of more and more of the realities of wealth from private hands and, in exchange, the contracting of great masses of debt to private people. The nett tendency is towards the disappearance of a reality holding class and the destruction of realities in warfare, and the appearance of a vast *rentier* class in its place. At the end of the war much material will be destroyed for evermore, transit, food production and industry will be everywhere enormously socialised, and the country will be liable to pay every year in interest, a sum of money exceeding the entire national expenditure before the war. From the point of view of the state, and disregarding material and moral damages, that annual interest is the annual instalment of the price to be paid for the war.

Now the interesting question arises whether these great belligerent states may go bankrupt, and if so to what extent. States may go bankrupt to the private creditor without repudiating their debts or seeming to pay less to him. They can go bankrupt either by a depreciation of their currency or—without touching the gold standard—through a rise in prices. In the end both these things work out to the same end; the creditor gets so many loaves or pairs of boots or workman's hours of labour for his pound *less* than he would have got under the previous conditions. One may imagine this process of price (and of course wages) increase going on to a limitless extent. Many people are inclined to look to such an increase in prices as a certain outcome of the war, and just so far as it goes, just so far will the burthen of the *rentier* class, their call, tat is, for goods and services, be lightened. This expectation is very generally entertained, and I can see little reason against it. The intensely stupid or dishonest "labour" press, however, which in the interests of the common enemy misrepresents socialism and seeks to misguide labour in Great Britain, ignores these considerations, and positively holds out this prospect of rising prices as an alarming one to the more credulous and ignorant of its readers.

But now comes the second way of meeting the after-the-war obligations. This second way is by increasing the wealth of the state and by increasing the national production to such an extent that the payment of the *rentier* class will not be an overwhelming burthen. Rising prices bilk the creditor. Increased production will check the rise in prices and get him a real payment. The outlook for the national creditor seems to be that he will be partly bilked and partly paid; how far he will be bilked and how far depends almost entirely upon this possible increase in production; and there is consequently a very keen and quite unprecedented desire very widely diffused among intelligent and active people, holding War Loan scrip and the like, in all the belligerent countries, to see bold and hopeful schemes for state enrichment pushed forward. The movement towards socialism is receiving an impulse from a new and unexpected quarter, there is now a *rentier* socialism, and it is interesting to note that while the London *Times* is full of schemes of great state enterprises, for the exploitation of Colonial state lands, for the state purchase and wholesaling of food and many natural products, and for the syndication of shipping and the great staple industries into vast trusts into which not only the British but the French and Italian governments may enter as partners, the so-called socialist press of Great

Britain is chiefly busy about the draughts in the cell of Mr. Fenner Brockway and the refusal of Private Scott Duckers to put on his khaki trousers. *The New Statesman* and the Fabian Society, however, display a wider intelligence.

There is a great variety of suggestions for this increase of public wealth and production. Many of them have an extreme reasonableness. The extent to which they will be adopted depends, no doubt, very largely upon the politician and permanent official, and both these classes are prone to panic in the presence of reality. In spite of its own interests in restraining a rise in prices, the old official "salariat" is likely to be obstructive to any such innovations. It is the resistance of spurs and red tabs to military innovations over again. This is the resistance of quills and red tape. On the other hand the organisation of Britain for war has "officialised" a number of industrial leaders, and created a large body of temporary and adventurous officials. They may want to carry on into peace production the great new factories the war has created. At the end of the war, for example, every belligerent country will be in urgent need of cheap automobiles for farmers, tradesmen, and industrial purposes generally, America is now producing such automobiles at a price of eighty pounds. But Europe will be heavily in debt to America, her industries will be disorganised, and there will therefore be no sort of return payment possible for these hundreds of thousands of automobiles. A country that is neither creditor nor producer cannot be an importer. Consequently though those cheap tin cars may be stacked as high as the Washington Monument in America, they will never come to Europe. On the other hand the great shell factories of Europe will be standing idle and ready, their staffs disciplined and available, for conversion to the new task. The imperative common sense of the position seems to be that the European governments should set themselves straight away to out-Ford Ford, and provide their own people with cheap road transport.

But here comes in the question whether this common-sense course is inevitable. Suppose the mental energy left in Europe after the war is insufficient for such a constructive feat as this. There will certainly be the obstruction of official pedantry, the hold-up of this vested interest and that, the greedy desire of "private enterprise" to exploit the occasion upon rather more costly and less productive lines, the general distrust felt by ignorant and unimaginative people of a new way of doing things. The process after all may not get done in the obviously wise way. This will not mean that Europe will buy American cars. It will be quite unable to buy American cars. It will be unable to make anything that America will not be able to make more cheaply for itself. But it will mean that Europe will go on without cheap cars, that is to say it will go on a more sluggishly and clumsily and wastefully at a lower economic level. Hampered transport means hampered production of other things, and in increasing inability to buy abroad. And so we go down and down.

It does not follow that because a course is the manifestly right and advantageous course for the community that it will be taken. I am reminded of this by a special basket in my study here, into which I pitch letters, circulars, pamphlets and so forth as they come to hand from a gentleman named Gattie, and his friends Mr. Adrian Ross, Mr. Roy Horniman, Mr. Henry Murray and others. His particular project is the construction of a Railway Clearing House for London. It is an absolutely admirable scheme. It would cut down the heavy traffic in the streets of London to about one-third; it would enable us to run the goods traffic of England with less than half the number of railway trucks we now employ; it would turn over enormous areas of valuable land from their present use as railway goods yards and sidings; it would save time in the transit of goods and labour in their handling. It is a quite beautifully worked out scheme. For the last eight or ten years this group of devoted fanatics has been pressing this undertaking upon an indifferent country with increasing vehemence and astonishment at that indifference. The point is that its adoption, though it would be of general benefit, would be of no particular benefit to any leading man or highly placed official. On the other hand it would upset all sorts of individuals who are in a position to obstruct it quietly—and they do so. Meaning no evil. I dip my hand in the accumulation and extract a leaflet by the all too zealous Mr. Murray. In it he denounces various public officials by name as he cheats and scoundrels, and invites a prosecution for libel.

In that fashion nothing will ever get done. There is no prosecution, but for all that I do not agree with Mr. Murray about the men he names. These gentlemen are just comfortable gentlemen, own brothers to these old generals of ours who will not take off their spurs. They are probably quite charming people except that they know nothing of that Fear of God which searches by heart. Why should they bother?

So many of these after-the-war problems bring one back to the question of how far the war has put the Fear of God into the hearts of responsible men. There is really no other reason in existence that I can imagine why they should ask themselves the question, "Have I done my best?" and that still more important question, "Am I doing my best now?" And so while I hear plenty of talk about the great reorganisations that are to come after the war, while there is the stir of doubt among the *rentiers* whether, after all, they will get paid, while the unavoidable stresses and sacrifices of the war are making many people question the rightfulness of much that they did as a matter of course, and of much that they took for granted, I perceive there is also something dull and not very articulate in this European world, something resistant and inert, that is like the obstinate rolling over of a heavy sleeper after he has been called upon to get up. "Just a little longer.... Just for *my* time."

One thought alone seems to make these more intractable people anxious. I thrust it in as my last stimulant when everything else has failed. "There will be *frightful* trouble with labour after the war," I say.

They try to persuade themselves that military discipline is breaking in labour....

2

What does British labour think of the outlook after the war?

As a distinctive thing British labour does not think. "Class-conscious labour," as the Marxists put it, scarcely exists in Britain. The only convincing case I ever met was a bath-chairman of literary habits Eastbourne. The only people who are, as a class, class-conscious in the British community are the Anglican gentry and their fringe of the genteel. Everybody else is "respectable." The mass of British workers find their thinking in the ordinary halfpenny papers or in *John Bull*. The so-called labour papers are perhaps less representative of British Labour than any other section of the press; the *Labour Leader*, for example, is the organ of such people as Bertrand Russell, Vernon Lee, Morel, academic *rentiers* who know about as much of the labour side of industrialism as they do of cock-fighting. All the British peoples are racially willing and good-tempered people, quite ready to be led by those they imagine to be abler than themselves. They make the most cheerful and generous soldiers in the whole world, without insisting upon that democratic respect which the Frenchman exacts. They do not criticise and they do not trouble themselves much about the general plan of operations, so long as they have confidence in the quality and good will of their leading. But British soldiers will of their loading. But British soldiers will hiss a general when they think he is selfish, unfeeling, or a muff. And the socialist propaganda has imported ideas of public service into private employment. Labour in Britain has been growing increasingly impatient of bad or selfish industrial leadership. Labour trouble in Great Britain turns wholly upon the idea crystallised in the one word "profiteer." Legislation and regulation of hours of labour, high wages, nothing will keep labour quiet in Great Britain if labour thinks it is being exploited for private gain.

Labour feels very suspicious of private gain. For that suspicion a certain rather common type of employer is mainly to blame. Labour believes that employers is mainly to blame. Labour believes that employers as a class cheat workmen as a class, plan to cheat them of their full share in the common output, and drive hard bargains. It believes that private employers are equally ready to sacrifice the welfare of the nation and the welfare of the workers for mere personal advantage. It has a traditional experience to support these suspicions.

In no department of morals have ideas changed so completely during the last eight years as in relation to "profits". Eighty years ago everyone believed in the divine right of property to do what it pleased its advantages, a doctrine more disastrous socially than the divine right of kings. There was no such sense of the immorality of "holding up" as pervades the public conscience to-day. The worker was expected not only to work, but to be grateful for employment. The property owner held his property and handed it out for use and development or not, just as he thought fit. These ideas are not altogether extinct today. Only a few days ago I met a magnificent old lady of seventy nine or eighty, who discoursed upon the wickedness of her gardener in demanding another shilling a week because of war prices.

She was a valiant and handsome personage. A face that had still a healthy natural pinkness looked out from under blond curls, and an elegant and carefully tended hand tossed back some fine old lace to gesticulate more freely. She had previously charmed her hearers by sweeping aside certain rumours that were drifting about.

"Germans invade *Us!*" she cried. "Who'd *let* 'em, I'd like to know? Who'd *let* 'em?"

And then she reverted to her grievance about the gardener.

"I told him that after the war he'd be glad enough to get anything. Grateful! They'll all be coming back after the war—all of 'em, glad enough to get anything. Asking for another shilling indeed!"

Everyone who heard her looked shocked. But that was the tone of everyone of importance in the dark years that followed the Napoleonic wars. That is just one survivor of the old tradition. Another is Blight the solicitor, who goes about bewailing the fact that we writers are "holding out false hopes of higher agricultural wages after the war." But these are both exceptions. They are held to be remarkable people even by their own class. The mass of property owners and influential people in Europe to-day no more believe in the sacred right of property to hold up development and dictate terms than do the more intelligent workers. The ideas of collective ends and of the fiduciary nature of property, had been soaking through the European community for years before the war. The necessity for sudden and even violent co-operations and submersions of individuality in a common purpose, is rapidly crystallising out these ideas into clear proposals.

War is an evil thing, but most people who will not learn from reason must have an ugly teacher. This war has brought home to everyone the supremacy of the public need over every sort of individual claim.

One of the most remarkable things in the British war press is the amount of space given to the discussion of labour developments after the war. This in its completeness peculiar to the British situation. Nothing on the same scale is perceptible in the press of the Latin allies. A great movement on the part of capitalists and business organisers is manifest to assure the worker of a change of heart and a will to change method. Labour is suspicious, not foolishly but wisely suspicious. But labour is considering it.

"National industrial syndication," say the business organisers.

"Guild socialism," say the workers.

There is also a considerable amount of talking and writing about "profit-sharing" and about giving the workers a share in the business direction. Neither of these ideas appeals to the shrewder heads among the workers. So far as direction goes their disposition is to ask the captain to command the ship. So far as profits go, they think the captain has no more right than the cabin boy to speculative gains; he should do his work for his pay whether it is profitable or unprofitable work. There is little balm for labour discontent in these schemes for making the worker also an infinitesimal profiteer.

During my journey in Italy and France I met several men who were keenly interested in business organisation. Just before I started my friend N, who has been the chief partner in the building up of a very big and very extensively advertised American business, came to see me on his way back to America. He is as interested in his work as a scientific specialist, and as ready to talk about it to any intelligent and interested hearer. He was particularly keen upon the question of continuity in the business, when it behoves the older generation to let in the younger to responsible management and to efface themselves. He was a man of five-and-forty. Incidentally he mentioned that he had never taken anything for his private life out of the great business he had built up but a salary, "a good salary," and that now he was gong to grant himself a pension. "I shan't interfere any more. I shall come right away and live in Europe for a year so as not to be tempted to interfere. The boys have got to run it some day, and they had better get their experience while they're young and capable of learning by it. I did."

I like N's ideas. "Practically," I said, "you've been a public official. You've treated your business like a public service."

That was his idea.

"Would you mind if it was a public service?"

He reflected, and some disagreeable memory darkened his face. "Under the politicians?" he said.

I took the train of thought N had set going abroad with me next day. I had the good luck to meet men who were interesting industrially. Captain Pirelli, my guide in Italy, has a name familiar to every motorist; his name goes wherever cars go, spelt with a big long capital P. Lieutenant de Tessin's name will recall one of the most interesting experiments in profit-sharing to the student of social science. I tried over N's problem on both of them. I found in both their minds just the same attitude as he takes up towards his business. They think any businesses that are worthy of respect, the sorts of businesses that interest them, are public functions. Money-lenders and speculators, merchants and gambling gentlefolk may think in terms of profit; capable business directors certainly do nothing of the sort.

I met a British officer in France who is also a landowner. I got him to talk about his administrative work upon his property. He was very keen upon new methods. He said he tried to do his duty by his land.

"How much land?" I asked.

"Just over nine thousand acres," he said.

"But you could manage forty or fifty thousand with little more trouble."

"If I had it. In some ways it would be easier."

"What a waste!" I said. "Of course you ought not to *own* these acres; what you ought to be is the agricultural controller of just as big an estate of the public lands as you could manage—with a suitable salary."

He reflected upon that idea. He said he did not get much of a salary out of his land as it was, and made a regrettable allusion to Mr. Lloyd George. "When a man tries to do his duty by his land," he said...

But here running through the thoughts of the Englishman and the Italian and the Frenchman and the American alike one finds just the same idea of a kind of officialdom in ownership. It is an idea that pervades our thought and public discussion to-day everywhere, and it is an idea that is scarcely traceable at all in the thought of the early half of the nineteenth century. The idea of service and responsibility in property has increased and is increasing, the conception of "hold-up," the usurer's conception of his right to be bought out of the way, fades. And the process has been enormously enhanced by the various big-scale experiments in temporary socialism that have been forced upon the belligerent powers. Men of the most individualistic quality are being educated up to the possibilities of concerted collective action. My friend and fellow-student Y, inventor and business organiser, who used to make the best steam omnibuses in the world, and who is now making all sorts of things for the army, would go pink with suspicious anger at the mere words "inspector" or "socialism" three or four years ago. He does not do so now.

A great proportion of this sort of man, this energetic directive sort of man in England, is thinking socialism to-day. They may not be saying socialism, but they are thinking it. When labour begins to realise what is adrift it will be divided between two things: between appreciative co-operation, for which guild socialism in particular has prepared its mind, and traditional suspicion. I will not over to guess here which will prevail.

3

The impression I have of the present mental process in the European communities is that while the official class and the *rentier* class is thinking very poorly and inadequately and with a merely obstructive disposition; while the churches are merely wasting their energies in futile self-advertisement; while the labour mass is suspicious and disposed to make terms for itself rather than come into any large schemes of reconstruction that will abolish profit as a primary aim in economic life, there is still a very considerable movement towards such a reconstruction. Nothing is so misleading as a careless analogy. In the dead years that followed the Napoleonic wars, which are often quoted as a precedent for expectation now, the spirit of collective service was near its minimum; it was never so strong and never so manifestly spreading and increasing as it is to-day.

But service to what?

I have my own very strong preconceptions here, and since my temperament is sanguine they necessarily colour my view. I believe that this impulse to collective service can satisfy itself only under the formula that mankind is one state of which God is the undying king, and that the service of men's collective needs is the true worship of God. But eagerly as I would grasp at any evidence that this idea is being developed and taken up by the general consciousness, I am quite unable to persuade myself that anything of the sort is going on. I do perceive a search for large forms into which the prevalent impulse to devotion can be thrown. But the organised religious bodies, with their creeds and badges and their instinct for self-preservation at any cost, stand between men and their spiritual growth in just the same way the forestallers stand between men and food. Their activities at present are an almost intolerable nuisance. One cannot say "God" but some tout is instantly seeking to pluck one into his particular cave of flummery and orthodoxy. What a rational man means by God is just God. The more you define and argue about God the more he remains the same simple thing.

Judaism, Christianity, Islam, modern Hindu religious thought, all agree in declaring that there is one God, master and leader of all mankind, in unending conflict with cruelty, disorder, folly and waste. To my mind, it follows immediately that there can be no king, no government of any sort, which is not either a subordinate or a rebel government, a local usurpation, in the kingdom of God. But no organised religious body has ever had the courage and honesty to insist upon this. They all pander to nationalism and to powers and princes. They exists so to pander. Every organised religion in the world exists only to exploit and divert and waste the religious impulse in man.

This conviction that the world kingdom of God is the only true method of human service, is so clear and final in my own mind, it seems so inevitably the conviction to which all right-thinking men must ultimately come, that I feel almost like a looker-on at a game of blind-man's bluff as I watch the discussion of synthetic political ideas. The blind man thrusts his seeking hands into the oddest corners, he clutches at chairs and curtains, but at last he must surely find and hold and feel over and guess the name of the plainly visible quarry.

Some of the French and Italian people I talked to said they were fighting for "Civilisation." That is one name for the kingdom of God, and I have heard English people use it too. But much of the contemporary thought of England stills wanders with its back to the light. Most of it is pawing over jerry-built, secondary things. I have before me a little book, the joint work of Dr. Grey and Mr. Turner, of an ex-public schoolmaster and a manufacturer, called *Eclipse or Empire?* (The title *World Might or Downfall?* had already been secured in another quarter.) It is a book that has been enormously advertised; it has been almost impossible to escape its column-long advertisements; it is billed upon the hoardings, and it is on the whole a very able and right-spirited book. It calls for more and better education, for more scientific methods, for less class suspicion and more social explicitness and understanding, for a franker and fairer treatment of labour. But why does it call for these things? Does it call for them because they are right? Because in accomplishing them one serves God?

Not at all. But because otherwise this strange sprawling empire of ours will drop back into a secondary place in the world. These two writers really seem to think that the slack workman, the slacker wealthy man, the negligent official, the conservative schoolmaster, the greedy usurer, the comfortable obstructive, confronted with this alternative, terrified at this idea of something or other called the Empire being "eclipsed," eager for the continuance of this undefined glory over their fellow-creatures called "Empire," will perceive the error of their ways and become energetic, devoted, capable. They think an ideal of that sort is going to change the daily lives of men.... I sympathise with their purpose, and I deplore their conception of motives. If men will not give themselves for righteousness, they will not give themselves for a geographical score. If they will not work well for the hatred of bad work, they will not work well for the hatred of Germans. This "Empire" idea has been cadging about the British empire, trying to collect enthusiasm and devotion, since the days of Disraeli. It is, I submit, too big for the mean-spirited, and too tawdry and limited for the fine and generous. It leaves out the French and the Italians and the Belgians and all our blood brotherhood of allies. It has no compelling force in it. We British are not naturally Imperialist; we are something greater—or something less. For two years and a half now we have been fighting against Imperialism in its most extravagant form. It is a poor incentive to right living to propose to parody the devil we fight against.

The blind man must lunge again.

For when the right answer is seized it answers not only the question why men should work for their fellow-men but also why nation should cease to arm and plan and contrive against nation. The social problem is only the international problem in retail, the international problem is only the social one in gross.

My bias rules me altogether here. I see men in social, in economic and in international affairs alike, eager to put an end to conflict, inexpressibly weary of conflict and the waste and pain and death it involves. But to end conflict one must abandon aggressive or uncordial pretensions. Labour is sick at the idea of more strikes and struggles after the war, industrialism is sick of competition and anxious for service, everybody is sick of war. But how can they end any of these clashes except by the definition and recognition of a common end which will establish a standard for the trial of every conceivable issue, to which, that is, every other issue can be subordinated; and what common end can there be in all the world except this idea of the world kingdom of God? What is the good of orienting one's devotion to a firm, or to class solidarity, or *La Republique Francais*, or Poland, or Albania, or such love and loyalty as people profess for King George or King Albert or the Duc d'Orleans—it puzzles me why—or any such intermediate object of self-abandonment? We need a standard so universal that the platelayer may say to the barrister or the duchess, or the Red Indian to the Limehouse sailor, or the Anzac soldier to the Sinn Feiner or the Chinaman, "What are we two doing for it?" And to fill the place of that "it," no other idea is great enough or commanding enough, but only the world kingdom of God.

However long he may have to hunt, the blind man who is seeking service and an end to bickerings will come to that at last, because of all the thousand other things he may clutch at, nothing else can satisfy his manifest need.

VI. THE ENDING OF THE WAR

1

About the end of the war there are two chief ways of thinking, there is a simpler sort of mind which desires merely a date, and a more complex kind which wants particulars. To the former class belong most of the men out at the front. They are so bored by this war that they would welcome any peace that did not definitely admit defeat—and examine the particulars later. The "tone" of the German army, to judge by its captured letters, is even lower. It would welcome peace in any form. Never in the whole history of the world has a war been so universally unpopular as this war.

The mind of the soldier is obsessed by a vision of home-coming for good, so vivid and alluring that it blots out nearly every other consideration. The visions of people at home are of plenty instead of privation, lights up, and the cessation of a hundred tiresome restrictions. And it is natural therefore that a writer rather given to guesses and forecasts should be asked very frequently to guess how long the war has still to run.

All such forecasting is the very wildest of shooting. There are the chances of war to put one out, and of a war that changes far faster than the military intelligence. I have made various forecasts. At the outset I thought that military Germany would fight at about the 1899 level, would be lavish with cavalry and great attacks, that it would be reluctant to entrench, and that the French and British had learnt the lesson of the Boer war better than the Germans. I trusted to the melodramatic instinct of the Kaiser. I trusted to the quickened intelligence of the British military caste. The first rush seemed to bear me out, and I opened my paper day by day expecting to read of the British and French entrenched and the Germans beating themselves to death against wire and trenches. In those days I wrote of the French being over the Rhine before 1915. But it was the Germans who entrenched first.

Since then I have made some other attempts. I did not prophesy at all in 1915, so far as I can remember. If I had I should certainly have backed the Gallipoli attempt to win. It was the right thing to do, and it was done abominably. It should have given us Constantinople and brought Bulgaria to our side; it gave us a tragic history of administrative indolence and negligence, and wasted bravery and devotion. I was very hopeful of the western offensive in 1915; and in 1916 I counted still on our continuing push. I believe we were very near something like decision this last September, but some archaic dream of doing it with cavalry dashed these hopes. The "Tanks" arrived to late to do their proper work, and their method of use is being worked out very slowly.... I still believe in the western push, if only we push it for all we are worth. If only we push it with our brains, with our available and still unorganised brains; if only we realise that the art of modern war is to invent and invent and invent. Hitherto I have always hoped and looked for decision, a complete victory that would enable the Allies to dictate peace. But such an expectation is largely conditioned by these delicate questions of adaptability that my tour of the front has made very urgent in my mind. A spiteful German American writer has said that the British would rather kill twenty thousand of their men than break one general. Even a grain of truth in such a remark is a very valid reasoning for lengthening one's estimate of the duration of the war.

There can be no doubt that the Western allies are playing a winning game upon the western front, and that this is the front of decision now. It is not in doubt that they are beating the Germans and shoving them back. The uncertain factor is the rate at which they are shoving them back. If they can presently get to so rapid an advance as to bring the average rate since July 1st up to two or three miles a day, then we shall still see the Allies dictating terms. But if the shove drags on at its present pace of less than a mile and four thousand prisoners a week over the limited Somme front only, if nothing is attempted elsewhere to increase the area of pressure, [*This was written originally before the French offensive at Verdun.] then the intolerable stress and boredom of the war will bring about a peace long before the Germans are decisively crushed. But the war, universally detested, may go on into 1918 or 1919. Food riots, famine, and general disorganisation will come before 1920, if it does. The Allies have a winning game before them, but they seem unable to discover and promote the military genius needed to harvest an unquestionable victory. In the long run this may not be an unmixed evil. Victory, complete and dramatic, may be bought too dearly. We need not triumphs out of this war but the peace of the world.

This war is altogether unlike any previous war, and its ending, like its development, will follow a course of its own. For a time people's minds ran into the old grooves, the Germans were going *nach Paris* and *nach London*; Lord Curzon filled our minds with a pleasant image of the Bombay Lancers riding down *Unter den Linden*. But the Versailles precedent of a council of victors dictating terms to the vanquished is not now so evidently in men's minds. The utmost the Allies talk upon now is to say, "We must end the war on German soil." The Germans talk frankly of "holding out." I have guessed that the western offensive will be chiefly on German soil by next June; it is a mere guess, and I admit it is quite conceivable that the "push" may still be grinding out its daily tale of wounded and prisoners in 1918 far from that goal.

None of the combatants expected such a war as this, and the consequence is that the world at large has no idea how to get out of it. The war may stay with us like a schoolboy caller, because it does not know how to go. The Italians said as much to me. "Suppose we get to Innsbruck and Laibach and Trieste," they said, "it isn't an end!" Lord Northcliffe, I am told, came away from Italy with the conviction that the war would last six years.

There is the clearest evidence that nearly everyone is anxious to get out of the war now. Nobody at all, except perhaps a few people who may be called to account, and a handful of greedy profit-seekers, wants to keep it going. Quietly perhaps and unobtrusively, everyone I know is now trying to find the way out of the war, and I am convinced that the same is the case in Germany. That is what makes the Peace-at-any-price campaign so exasperating. It is like being chased by clamorous geese across a common in the direction in which you want to go. But how are we to get out—with any credit—in such a way as to prevent a subsequent collapse into another war as frightful?

At present three programmes are before the world of the way in which the war can be ended. The first of these assumes a complete predominance of our Allies. It has been stated in general terms by Mr. Asquith. Evacuation, reparation, due punishment of those responsible for the war, and guarantees that nothing of the sort shall happen again. There is as yet no mention of the nature of these guarantees. Just exactly what is to happen to Poland, Austria, and the Turkish Empire does not appear in this prospectus. The German Chancellor is equally elusive. The Kaiser has stampeded the peace-at-any-price people of Great Britain by proclaiming that Germany wants peace. We knew that. But what sort of peace? It would seem that we are promised vaguely evacuation and reparation on the western frontier, and in addition there are to be guarantees—but it is quite evident that they are altogether different guarantees from Mr. Asquith's— that nothing of the sort is ever to happen again. The programme of the British and their Allies seems to contemplate something like a forcible disarmament and military occupation of Belgium, the desertion of Serbia and Russia, and the surrender to Germany of every facility for a later and more successful German offensive in the west. But it is clear that on these terms as stated the war must go on to the definite defeat of one side or the other, or a European chaos. They are irreconcilable sets of terms.

Yet it is hard to say how they can be modified on either side, if the war is to be decided only between the belligerents and by standards of national interest only, without reference to any other considerations. Our Allies would be insane to leave the Hohenzollern at the end of the war with a knife in his hand, after the display he has made of his quality. To surrender his knife means for the Hohenzollern the abandonment of his dreams, the repudiation of the entire education and training of Germany for half a century. When we realise the fatality of this antagonism, we realise how it is that, in this present anticipation of hell, the weary, wasted and tormented nations must still sustain their monstrous dreary struggle. And that is why this thought that possible there may be a side way out, a sort of turning over of the present endlessly hopeless game into a new and different and manageable game through the introduction of some external factor, creeps and spreads as I find it creeping and spreading.

That is what the finer intelligences of America are beginning to realise, and why men in Europe continually turn their eyes to America, with a surmise, with a doubt.

A point of departure for very much thinking in this matter is the recent speech of President Wilson that heralded the present discussion. All Europe was impressed by the truth, and by President Wilson's recognition of the truth, that from any other great war after this America will be unable to abstain. Can America come into this dispute at the end to insist upon something better than a new diplomatic patchwork, and so obviate the later completer Armageddon? Is there, above the claims and passions of Germany, France, Britain, and the rest of them, a conceivable right thing to do for all mankind, that it might also be in the interest of America to support? Is there a Third Party solution, so to speak, which may possibly be the way out from this war?

And further I would go on to ask, is not this present exchange of Notes, appealing to the common sense of the world, really the beginning, and the proper beginning, of the unprecedented Peace Negotiations to end this unprecedented war? And, I submit, the longer this open discussion goes on before the doors close upon the secret peace congress the better for mankind.

2

Let me sketch out here what I conceive to be the essentials of a world settlement. Some of the items are the mere commonplaces of everyone who discusses this question; some are less frequently insisted upon. I have been joining up one thing to another, suggestions I have heard from this man and that, and I believe that it is really possible to state a solution that will be acceptable to the bulk of reasonable men all about the world. Directly we put the panic-massacres of Dinant and Louvain, the crime of the *Lusitania* and so on into the category of symptoms rather than essentials, outrages that call for special punishments and reparations, but that do not enter further into the ultimate settlement, we can begin to conceive a possible world treaty. Let me state the broad outlines of this pacification. The outlines depend one upon the other; each is a condition of the other. It is upon these lines that the thoughtful, as distinguished from the merely the combative people, seem to be drifting everywhere.

In the first place, it is agreed that there would have to be an identical treaty between all the great powers of the world binding them to certain things. It would have to provide:—

That the few great industrial states capable of producing modern war equipment should take over and control completely the manufacture of all munitions of war in the world. And that they should absolutely close the supply of such material to all the other states in the world. This is a far easier task than many people suppose. War has now been so developed on its mechanical side that the question of its continuance or abolition rests now entirely upon four or five great powers.

Next comes the League of Peace idea; that there should be an International Tribunal for the discussion and settlement of international disputes. That the dominating powers should maintain land and sea forces only up to a limit agreed upon and for internal police use only or for the purpose of enforcing the decisions of the Tribunal. That they should all be bound to attack and suppress any power amongst them which increases its war equipment beyond its defined limits.

That much has already been broached in several quarters. But so far is not enough. It ignores the chief processes of that economic war that aids and abets and is inseparably a part of modern international conflicts. If we are to go as far as we have already stated in the matter of international controls, then we must go further and provide that the International Tribunal should have power to consider and set aside all tariffs and localised privileges that seem grossly unfair or seriously irritating between the various states of the world. It should have power to pass or revise all new tariff, quarantine, alien exclusion, or the like legislation affecting international relations. Moreover, it should take over and extend the work of the International Bureau of Agriculture at Rome with a view to the control of all staple products. It should administer the sea law of the world, and control and standardise freights in the common interests of mankind. Without these provisions it would be merely preventing the use of certain weapons; it would be doing nothing to prevent countries strangling or suffocating each other by commercial warfare. It would not abolish war.

Now upon this issue people do not seem to me to be yet thinking very clearly. It is the exception to find anyone among the peace talkers who really grasps how inseparably the necessity for free access for everyone to natural products, to coal and tropical products, e.g. free shipping at non-discriminating tariffs, and the recognition by a Tribunal of the principle of common welfare in trade matters, is bound up with the ideal of a permanent world peace. But any peace that does not provide for these things will be merely laying down of the sword in order to take up the cudgel. And a "peace" that did not rehabilitate industrial Belgium, Poland, and the north of France would call imperatively for the imposition upon the Allies of a system of tariffs in the interests of these countries, and for a bitter economic "war after the war" against Germany. That restoration is, of course, an implicit condition to any attempt to set up an economic peace in the world.

These things being arranged for the future, it would be further necessary to set up an International Boundary Commission, subject to certain defining conditions agreed upon by the belligerents, to re-draw the map of Europe, Asia, and Africa. This war does afford an occasion such as the world may never have again of tracing out the "natural map" of mankind, the map that will secure the maximum of homogeneity and the minimum of racial and economic freedom. All idealistic people hope for a restored Poland. But it is a childish thing to dream of a contented Poland with Posen still under the Prussian heel, with Cracow cut off, and without a Baltic port. These claims of Poland to completeness have a higher sanction than the mere give and take of belligerents in congress.

Moreover this International Tribunal, if it was indeed to prevent war, would need also to have power to intervene in the affairs of any country or region in a state of open and manifest disorder, for the protection of foreign travellers and of persons and interests localised in that country but foreign to it.

Such an agreement as I have here sketched out would at once lift international politics out of the bloody and hopeless squalor of the present conflict. It is, I venture to assert, the peace of the reasonable man in any country whatever. But it needs the attention of such a disengaged people as the American people to work it out and supply it with—weight. It needs putting before the world with some sort of authority greater than its mere entire reasonableness. Otherwise it will not come before the minds of ordinary men with the effect of a practicable proposition. I do not see any such plant springing from the European battlefields. It is America's supreme opportunity. And yet it is the common sense of the situation, and the solution that must satisfy a rational German as completely as a rational Frenchman or Englishman. It has nothing against it but the prejudice against new and entirely novel things.

3

In throwing out the suggestion that America should ultimately undertake the responsibility of proposing a world peace settlement, I admit that I run counter to a great deal of European feeling. Nowhere in Europe now do people seem to be in love with the United States. But feeling is a colour that passes. And the question is above matters of feeling. Whether the belligerents dislike Americans or the Americans dislike the belligerents is an incidental matter. The main question is of the duty of a great and fortunate nation towards the rest of the world and the future of mankind.

I do not know how far Americans are aware of the trend of feeling in Europe at the present time. Both France and Great Britain have a sense of righteousness in this war such as no nation, no people, has ever felt in war before. We know we are fighting to save all the world from the rule of force and the unquestioned supremacy of the military idea. Few Frenchmen or Englishmen can imagine the war presenting itself to an American intelligence under any other guise. At the invasion of Belgium we were astonished that America did nothing. At the sinking of the *Lusitania* all Europe looked to America. The British mind contemplates the spectacle of American destroyers acting as bottleholders to German submarines with a dazzled astonishment. "Manila," we gasp. In England we find excuses for America in our own past. In '64 we betrayed Denmark; in '70 we deserted France. The French have not these memories. They do not understand the damning temptations of those who feel they are "*au-dessus de la melee.*" They believe they had some share in the independence of America, that there is a sacred cause in republicanism, that there are grounds for a peculiar sympathy between France and the United States in republican institutions. They do not realise that Germany and America have a common experience in recent industrial development, and a common belief in the "degeneracy" of all nations with a lower rate of trade expansion. They do not realise how a political campaign with the slogan of "Peace and a Full Dinner-Pail" looks in the middle west, what an honest, simple, rational appeal it makes there. Atmospheres alter values. In Europe, strung up to tragic and majestic issues, to Europe gripping a gigantic evil in a death struggle, that would seem an inscription worthy of a pigsty. A child in Europe would know now that the context is, "until the bacon-buyer calls," and it is difficult to realise that adult citizens in America may be incapable of realising that obvious context.

I set these things down plainly. There is a very strong disposition in all the European countries to believe America fundamentally indifferent to the rights and wrongs of the European struggle; sentimentally interested perhaps, but fundamentally indifferent. President Wilson is regarded as a mere academic sentimentalist by a great number of Europeans. There is a very widespread disposition to treat America lightly and contemptuously, to believe that America, as one man put it to me recently, "hasn't the heart to do anything great or the guts to do anything wicked." There is a strong undercurrent of hostility therefore to the idea of America having any voice whatever in the final settlement after the war. It is not for a British writer to analyse the appearance that have thus affected American world prestige. I am telling what I have observed.

Let me relate two trivial anecdotes.

X came to my hotel in Paris one day to take me to see a certain munitions organisation. He took from his pocket a picture postcard that had been sent him by a well-meaning American acquaintance from America. It bore a portrait of General Lafayette, and under it was printed the words, "General Lafayette, *Colonel in the United States army.*"

"Oh! These Americans!" said X with a gesture.

And as I returned to Paris from the French front, our train stopped at some intermediate station alongside of another train of wounded men. Exactly opposite our compartment was a car. It arrested our conversation. It was, as it were, an ambulance *de grand luxe*; it was a thing of very light, bright wood and very golden decorations; at one end of it was painted very large and fair the Stars and Stripes, and at the other fair-sized letters of gold proclaimed—I am sure the lady will not resent this added gleam of publicity—"Presented by Mrs. William Vanderbilt."

My companions were French writers and French military men, and they were discussing with very keen interest that persistent question, "the ideal battery." But that ambulance sent a shaft of light into our carriage, and we stared together.

Then Colonel Z pointed with two fingers and remarked to us, without any excess of admiration:

"*America!*"

Then he shrugged his shoulders and pulled down the corners of his mouth.

We felt there was nothing more to add to that, and after a little pause the previous question was resumed.

I state these things in order to make it clear that America will start at a disadvantage when she starts upon the mission of salvage and reconciliation which is, I believe, her proper role in this world conflict. One would have to be blind and deaf on this side to be ignorant of European persuasion of America's triviality. I would not like to be an American travelling in Europe now, and those I meet here and there have some of the air of men who at any moment may be dunned for a debt. They explode without provocation into excuses and expostulations.

And I will further confess that when Viscount Grey answered the intimations of President Wilson and ex-President Taft of an American initiative to found a World League for Peace, by asking if America was prepared to back that idea with force, he spoke the doubts of all thoughtful European men. No one but an American deeply versed in the idiosyncrasies of the American population can answer that question, or tell us how far the delusion of world isolation which has prevailed in America for several generations has been dispelled. But if the answer to Lord Grey is "Yes," then I think history will emerge with a complete justification of the obstinate maintenance of neutrality by America. It is the end that reveals a motive. It is our ultimate act that sometimes teaches us our original intention. No one can judge the United States yet. Were you neutral because you are too mean and cowardly, or too stupidly selfish, or because you had in view an end too great to be sacrificed to a moment of indignant pride and a force in reserve too precious to dispel? That is the still open question for America.

Every country is a mixture of many strands. There is a Base America, there is a Dull America, there is an Ideal and Heroic America. And I am convinced that at present Europe underrates and misjudges the possibilities of the latter.

All about the world to-day goes a certain freemasonry of thought. It is an impalpable and hardly conscious union of intention. It thinks not in terms of national but human experience; it falls into directions and channels of thinking that lead inevitably to the idea of a world-state under the rule of one righteousness. In no part of the world is this modern type of mind so abundantly developed, less impeded by antiquated and perverse political and religious forms, and nearer the sources of political and administrative power, than in America. It does not seem to matter what thousand other things America may happen to be, seeing that it is also that. And so, just as I cling to the belief, in spite of hundreds of adverse phenomena, that the religious and social stir of these times must ultimately go far to unify mankind under the kingship of God, so do I cling also to the persuasion that there are intellectual forces among the rational elements in the belligerent centres, among the other neutrals and in America, that will co-operate in enabling the United States to play that role of the Unimpassioned Third Party, which becomes more and more necessary to a generally satisfactory ending of the war.

4

The idea that the settlement of this war must be what one might call an unimpassioned settlement or, if you will, a scientific settlement or a judicial and not a treaty settlement, a settlement, that is, based upon some conception of what is right and necessary rather than upon the relative success or failure of either set of belligerents to make its Will the standard of decision, is one that, in a great variety of forms and partial developments, I find gaining ground in the most different circles. The war was an adventure, it was the German adventure under the Hohenzollern tradition, to dominate the world. It was to be the last of the Conquests. It has failed. Without calling upon the reserve strength of America the civilised world has defeated it, and the war continues now partly upon the issue whether it shall be made for ever impossible, and partly because Germany has no organ but its Hohenzollern organisation through which it can admit its failure and develop its latent readiness for a new understanding on lines of mutual toleration. For that purpose nothing more reluctant could be devised than Hohenzollern imperialism. But the attention of every new combatant—it is not only Germany now—has been concentrated upon military necessities; every nation is a clenched nation, with its powers of action centred in its own administration, bound by many strategic threats and declarations, and dominated by the idea of getting and securing advantages. It is inevitable that a settlement made in a conference of belligerents alone will be shortsighted, harsh, limited by merely incidental necessities, and obsessed by the idea of hostilities and rivalries continuing perennially; it will be a trading of advantages for subsequent attacks. It will be a settlement altogether different in effect as well as in spirit from a world settlement made primarily to establish a new phase in the history of mankind.

Let me take three instances of the impossibility of complete victory *on either side* giving a solution satisfactory to the conscience and intelligence of reasonable men.

The first—on which I will not expatiate, for everyone knows of its peculiar difficulty—is Poland.

The second is a little one, but one that has taken hold of my imagination. In the settlement of boundaries preceding this war the boundary between Serbia and north-eastern Albania was drawn with an extraordinary disregard of the elementary needs of the Albanians of that region. It ran along the foot of the mountains which form their summer pastures and their refuge from attack, and it cut their mountains off from their winter pastures and market towns. Their whole economic life was cut to pieces and existence rendered intolerable for them. Now an intelligent Third Party settling

Europe would certainly restore these market towns, Ipek, Jakova, and Prisrend, to Albania. But the Albanians have no standing in this war; theirs is the happy lot that might have fallen to Belgium had she not resisted; the war goes to and fro through Albania; and when the settlement comes, it is highly improbable that the slightest notice will be taken of Albania's plight in the region. In which case these particular Albanians will either be driven into exile to America or they will be goaded to revolt, which will be followed no doubt by the punitive procedure usual in the Balkan peninsula.

For my third instance I would step from a matter as small as three market towns and the grazing of a few thousand head of sheep to a matter as big as the world. What is going to happen to the shipping of the world after this war? The Germans, with that combination of cunning and stupidity which baffles the rest of mankind, have set themselves to destroy the mercantile marine not merely of Britain and France but of Norway and Sweden, Holland, and all the neutral countries. The German papers openly boast that they are building up a big mercantile marine that will start out to take up the world's overseas trade directly peace is declared. Every such boast receives careful attention in the British press. We have heard a very great deal about the German will-to-power in this war, but there is something very much older and tougher and less blatant and conspicuous, the British will. In the British papers there has appeared and gained a permanent footing this phrase, "ton for ton." This means that Britain will go on fighting until she has exacted and taken over from Germany the exact equivalent of all the British shipping Germany has submarined. People do not realise that a time may come when Germany will be glad and eager to give Russia, France and Italy all that they require of her, when Great Britain may be quite content to let her allies make an advantageous peace and herself still go on fighting Germany. She does not intend to let that furtively created German mercantile marine ship or coal or exist upon the high seas—so long as it can be used as an economic weapon against her. Neither Britain nor France nor Italy can tolerate anything of the sort.

It has been the peculiar boast of Great Britain that her shipping has been unpatriotic. She has been the impartial carrier of the whole world. Her shippers may have served their own profit; they have never served hers. The fluctuations of freight charges may have been a universal nuisance, but they have certainly not been an aggressive national conspiracy. It is Britain's case against any German ascendancy at sea, an entirely convincing case, that such an ascendancy would be used ruthlessly for the advancement of German world power. The long-standing freedom of the seas vanishes at the German touch. So beyond the present war there opens the agreeable prospect of a mercantile struggle, a bitter freight war and a war of

Navigation Acts for the ultimate control in the interests of Germany or of the Anti-German allies, of the world's trade.

Now how in any of these three cases can the bargaining and trickery of diplomatists and the advantage-hunting of the belligerents produce any stable and generally beneficial solution? What all the neutrals want, what every rational and far-sighted man in the belligerent countries wants, what the common sense of the whole world demands, is neither the "ascendancy" of Germany nor the "ascendancy" of Great Britain nor the "ascendancy" of any state or people or interest in the shipping of the world. The plain right thing is a world shipping control, as impartial as the Postal Union. What right and reason and the welfare of coming generations demand in Poland is a unified and autonomous Poland, with Cracow, Danzig, and Posen brought into the same Polish-speaking ring-fence with Warsaw. What everyone who has looked into the Albanian question desires is that the Albanians shall pasture their flocks and market their sheepskins in peace, free of Serbian control. In every country at present at war, the desire of the majority of people is for a non-contentious solution that will neither crystallise a triumph nor propitiate an enemy, but which will embody the economic and ethnological and geographical common sense of the matter. But while the formulae of national belligerence are easy, familiar, blatant, and instantly present, the gentler, greater formulae of that wider and newer world pacifism has still to be generally understood. It is so much easier to hate and suspect than negotiate generously and patiently; it is so much harder to think than to let go in a shrill storm of hostility. The rational pacifist is hampered not only by belligerency, but by a sort of malignant extreme pacifism as impatient and silly as the extremest patriotism.

5

I sketch out these ideas of a world pacification from a third-party standpoint, because I find them crystallising out in men's minds. I note how men discuss the suggestion that America may play a large part in such a permanent world pacification. There I end my account rendered. These things are as much a part of my impression of the war as a shell-burst on the Carso or the yellow trenches at Martinpuich. But I do not know how opinion is going in America, and I am quite unable to estimate the power of these new ideas I set down, relative to the blind forces of instinct and tradition that move the mass of mankind. On the whole I believe more in the reason-guided will-power of men than I did in the early half of 1914. If I am doubtful whether after all this war will "end war," I think on the other hand it has had such an effect of demonstration that it may start a process of thought and conviction, it may sow the world with organisations and educational movements considerable enough to grapple with an either arrest or prevent the next great war catastrophe. I am by no means sure even now that this is not the last great war in the experience of men. I still believe it may be.

The most dangerous thing in the business so far is concerned is the wide disregard of the fact that national economic fighting is bound to cause war, and the almost universal ignorance of the necessity of subjecting shipping and overseas and international trade to some kind of international control. These two things, restraint of trade and advantage of shipping, are the chief material causes of anger between modern states. But they would not be in themselves dangerous things if it were not for the exaggerated delusions of kind and difference, and the crack-brained "loyalties" arising out of these, that seem still to rule men's minds. Years ago I came to the conviction that much of the evil in human life was due to the inherent vicious disposition of the human mind to intensify classification.[*See my "First and Last Things," Book I. and my "Modern Utopia," Chapter X.] I do not know how it will strike the reader, but to me this war, this slaughter of eight or nine million people, is due almost entirely to this little, almost universal lack of clear-headedness; I believe that the share of wickedness in making war is quite secondary to the share of this universal shallow silliness of outlook. These effigies of emperors and kings and statesmen that lead men into war, these legends of nationality and glory, would collapse before our universal derision, if they were not stuffed tight and full with the unthinking folly of the common man.

There is in all of us an indolent capacity for suffering evil and dangerous things, that I contemplate each year of my life with a deepening incredulity. I perceive we suffer them; I record the futile protests of the intelligence. It seems to me incredible that men should not rise up out of this muddy, bloody, wasteful mess of a world war, with a resolution to end for ever the shams, the prejudices, the pretences and habits that have impoverished their lives, slaughtered our sons, and wasted the world, a resolution so powerful and sustained that nothing could withstand it.

But it is not apparent that any such will arises. Does it appear at all? I find it hard to answer that question because my own answer varies with my mood. There are moods when it seems to me that nothing of the sort is happening. This war has written its warning in letters of blood and flame and anguish in the skies of mankind for two years and a half. When I look for the collective response to that warning, I see a multitude of little chaps crawling about their private ends like mites in an old cheese. The kings are still in their places, not a royal prince has been killed in this otherwise universal slaughter; when the fatuous portraits of the monarchs flash upon the screen the widows and orphans still break into loyal song. The ten thousand religions of mankind are still ten thousand religions, all busy at keeping men apart and hostile. I see scarcely a measurable step made anywhere towards that world kingdom of God, which is, I assert, the manifest solution, the only formula that can bring peace to all mankind. Mankind as a whole seems to have learnt nothing and forgotten nothing in thirty months of war.

And then on the other hand I am aware of much quiet talking. This book tells of how I set out to see the war, and it is largely conversation.... Perhaps men have always expected miracles to happen; if one had always lived in the night and only heard tell of the day, I suppose one would have expected dawn to come as a vivid flash of light. I suppose one would still think it was night long after the things about one had crept out of the darkness into visibility. In comparison with all previous wars there has been much more thinking and much more discussion. If most of the talk seems to be futile, if it seems as if everyone were talking and nobody doing, it does not follow that things are not quietly slipping and sliding out of their old adjustments amidst the babble and because of the babble. Multitudes of men must be struggling with new ideas. It is reasonable to argue that there must be reconsideration, there must be time, before these millions of mental efforts can develop into a new collective purpose and really *show*—in consequences.

But that they will do so is my hope always and, on the whole, except in moods of depression and impatience, my belief. When one has travelled to a conviction so great as mine it is difficult to doubt that other men faced by the same universal facts will not come to the same conclusion. I believe that only through a complete simplification o religion to its fundamental idea, to a world-wide realisation of God as the king of the heart and of all mankind, setting aside monarchy and national egotism altogether, can mankind come to any certain happiness and security. The precedent of Islam helps my faith in the creative inspiration of such a renascence of religion. The Sikh, the Moslem, the Puritan have shown that men can fight better for a Divine Idea than for any flag or monarch in the world. It seems to me that illusions fade and effigies lose credit everywhere. It is a very wonderful thing to me that China is now a republic.... I take myself to be very nearly an average man, abnormal only by reason of a certain mental rapidity. I conceive myself to be thinking as the world thinks, and if I find no great facts, I find a hundred little indications to reassure me that God comes. Even those who have neither the imagination nor the faith to apprehend God as a reality will, I think, realise presently that the Kingdom of God over a world-wide system of republican states, is the only possible formula under which we may hope to unify and save mankind.

www.ingramcontent.com/pod-product-compliance
Ingram Content Group UK Ltd.
Pitfield, Milton Keynes, MK11 3LW, UK
UKHW040449180225
455202UK00006B/386